A Wild Red River Tamed

A Brief History of the Colorado River and
Lake Powell

PETE KLOCKI AND TIFFANY MAPEL

A Wild Red River Tamed
A Brief History of the Colorado River and Lake Powell

iUniverse books may be ordered through booksellers or by contacting:

iUniverse
1663 Liberty Drive
Bloomington, IN 47403
www.iuniverse.com
844-349-9409

ISBN: 978-1-4401-8054-5 (sc)
ISBN: 978-1-4401-8055-2 (e)

Print information available on the last page.

iUniverse rev. date: 12/07/2021

Contents

"A man of wisdom delights in water."

~ Confucius

* Cover photograph of Gregory Butte and Colorado River
by R. G. Roth, 1963.

Foreword

"The flow of the river is ceaseless and its water is never the same. The bubbles that float in the pools, now vanishing, now forming, are not of long duration; so in the world are man and his dwellings... (People) die in the morning, they are born in the evening, like foam on the water."

~ Kamo Chomei (1153-1216), Hojo-Ki
(an account of my hut), 1212

For millions of years, the Colorado River has cut a swath through the sandstone of the Colorado Plateau. In the 20th century, man sought to control the raging red river. Today we have a veritable aquatic playground the entire length of its course. It alternates between river and lake, as it heads in the Rocky Mountains, and drains toward the Sea of Cortez. One has only to pick his or her favorite portion, and enjoy the waters of the Colorado.

Come along and learn some Colorado River history, and how man has contained and controlled the wild, red Colorado River. We'll take you through the canyons of Lake Powell and divulge their secrets. We'll even spend some time in the Grand Canyon—the Colorado's greatest achievement. Get to know the wild red river of the Colorado Plateau. And better yet, come visit the *Wild Red River* yourself in person.

*   *   *   *   *

The Colorado River's course is approximately 1,450 miles from its headwaters to the Sea of Cortez. It drains 242,900 square miles of arid regions on the Western Slope. In written records, the Spaniards first discovered the river in 1539. The river went through various names given by various explorers in the 1500s. In 1540, it was called "Rio del Tison." It was also called "Rio Colorado de los Martyres." An 1826 explorer known as Jedediah Smith called it the "Seedskeedee."

The Escalante expedition of 1776 labeled the river as "Colorado," and the San Juan River as "Nabajoo." Maps from that time label the Colorado River from its headwaters in Rocky Mountain National Park (elevation 9,010) as the "Grand River." When it joined with the Green River, it then became the Colorado. In 1921, at the request of the state of Colorado, the Grand River became known as the Colorado River.

Colorado River History

**A thumbnail history of the steps to contain and control
the Colorado River that leads to the creation
of fabulous Lake Powell.**

By Pete Klocki

"Water is a good servant, but it is a cruel master."

~ John Bullein, 1562

A tremendous family of mountain ranges called the "Continental Divide" splits the North American Continent into two major water drainages that profoundly affect the patterns and course of most North American rivers. This "spine" of America rises several thousand feet above sea level in places and precipitation in the form of rain or snow that falls on the east side of this divide flows to the Atlantic Ocean while water borne on the western side flows to the Pacific.

The rivers that carry these flows vary widely in character, temperament and personality, and the disparities between them are especially prominent when comparing the major western rivers with their eastern counterparts. Eastern rivers have served humankind nobly for centuries by supplying relatively reliable transportation corridors that allowed commerce to thrive and by also supplying a consistent and supremely adequate agricultural supporting water source. By historically providing both, the ability to grow food and cash farm crops, as well as a means to transport those crops to domestic and world markets, eastern rivers not only made important human development possible, but also allowed the American civil society to prosper.

And, for the most part, these benefits accrued to the people without the need to significantly alter or control the river systems. There were of course exceptions, but most eastern rivers prior to the onset of the industrial age were navigable in their natural state. The addition of levees, canals, locks, and other devices were manmade improvements installed primarily to increase the efficiency of waterborne transportation and to manage the spring runoff surge.

Western rivers, on the other hand, did not often lend themselves to eastern utilization models. And they still don't. Western rivers, by their inherent nature, are somewhat surly and uncooperative by comparison.

It isn't difficult to understand why that is so. Rivers that head at altitudes as high as fourteen thousand feet and plunge to the sea over relatively short horizontal distances might be expected to take on an excitable persona. And that description fits a great many of the rivers of the west.

In 1804, with an eye toward expanding the young nation's river commerce with the possible discovery of an inland water route to the Pacific, President Thomas Jefferson dispatched Captain Meriwether Lewis on an expedition designed to penetrate the Continental Divide and discover what lay beyond. But another fifty years would pass before explorers and scouts really began to open the country to westward expansion and develop an understanding of the challenges unique to the raw, untamed western third of the nation. And that, properly, is where our story begins.

There are four great river basin drainages west of the Continental Divide: the Columbia River Basin, the Pacific Coastal Basin, the Great Basin, and the Colorado River Basin. Early discoveries proved that the four were each unique in their own right, and in many instances bore little resemblance to each other.

Thanks to the foresight of Thomas Jefferson and the intrepid determination of Lewis and Clark, the Columbia River Basin was well known to Americans and to British fur traders at an early age. The settlement of Oregon and Washington followed relatively quickly. With the discovery of gold in California in 1849, the rivers of the Pacific Coastal Basin were explored at length within ten more years, and The Great Basin, centered on the Great Salt Lake in Northern Utah, was explored and Mormon settlement followed at about the same time.

The Colorado River Basin, though, was another matter. Any serious explorations of the southern half of the region that would explain the dynamics and challenges the namesake river presented were interrupted by the American Civil War's outbreak in 1861. Prior to that time, the vast open country south and east of the Colorado River was largely a hostile, unforgiving region whose natural obstacles to settlement were reinforced by dangerous Native American Indian tribes who guarded their territories against unwelcome encroachment with great determination. What's more, the river itself, "The Colorado," named by Spanish 16th Century explorers for its color, presented a bittersweet dilemma for early explorers and settlers. Although a Godsend in a hostile desert environment, its flow varied between a wintertime creek-like trickle to a roaring, red deluge during the springtime runoff floods. Shifting sands and rock-bottomed canyons made river commerce impossible. Reliable and safe crossings were few so that its very presence created an obstacle as effective as a stone wall to cross-country travel.

But the California gold rush provided incentive enough for man to begin considering the notion that the Colorado River might be transformed into something beyond an inconvenient nuisance.

In 1852, Fort Yuma was established on the California side of the river to watch over and provide protection at the "Yuma Crossing" on the river's lower reaches. A ferry at the site, established in 1850, had been a magnet for Indian confrontations that resulted in the violent loss of many lives. With the calming effect of the U.S. Army presence, cross-river operations became normalized. Soon explorers' eyes began to turn upriver ever more frequently.

Supplies to maintain Fort Yuma came from San Francisco by an impossibly inefficient water route that involved schooners sailing

3

south along the Pacific Coast to round the Southern tip of Baja and which then proceeded north the entire length of the Sea of Cortez to drop anchor off the Colorado River's delta. There, provisions and staple supply items were off-loaded onto flatboats that were then poled upriver against the current a variable distance of not less than some thirty-five miles. A clear necessity for a better way was obvious. Bread baked in San Francisco six weeks prior, was moldy and worm ridden by the time of its delivery to Fort Yuma.

In 1852 the first steamboat began to ply the river. It was the 65-foot long side-wheeler; The *Uncle Sam*, capable of carrying 32 tons of freight whose mission was to make transport between the river's mouth and Fort Yuma a far more efficient operation. This didn't work out, though.

Steamboat river travel was difficult at best. Shifting sands altered the river's channel on a daily basis, headway against the current limited upstream progress to no more than 15 miles a day, there was no coal for boiler fuel and the cutting of riverside trees was the only viable option. Wood cutting parties ashore were subject to frequent harassment by hostile Indians and if that were not enough, the skipper of the *Uncle Sam* relaxed his vigilance long enough one day in 1853 to run the boat hard aground.

Following that unhappy event, mule trains from San Diego accomplished supply deliveries to Fort Yuma for a period until replacement boats could be obtained and constructed. But in 1854, the first of three replacements, the *General Jessup*, was put into operation, quickly followed by two sternwheelers, the *Colorado* and the *Explorer*.

In 1858, Lieutenant Joseph C. Ives used the *Explorer* to conduct an upriver exploration that went to the limits of navigation at what was approximately the site of today's Hoover Dam at Black Canyon, and in 1859, Fort Mohave was established a short distance downstream from Ives' furthest explorations. That fort, using the Fort Yuma example, was also supplied by riverboat running against the river from the Gulf of California and that was pretty much how the situation remained until 1861.

With the outbreak of the Civil War that spring, settlement and exploration of the lower reaches of the Colorado River Basin essentially came to a halt. The emergency recall of Federal troops to counter the insurrection created a vacuum that allowed the Apache, Yuma, Mohave, Yavapai, Navajo and other tribes to reassert their dominance of the region. That situation did not begin to reverse itself until well after the Civil War's hostilities were concluded in 1865. But by then, with the discovery of fabulously rich mineral deposits scattered over the desert southwest, white Anglo settlement began in earnest.

The direction and extent of that wave of settlement would be determined by water, without which, existence in an extreme desert environment was impossible. Early on, settlement and agricultural development of the southwest tended to follow the path of least resistance. That is, the easy and the obvious had the greatest appeal to those who were more interested in making a living than experiencing adventure. Consequently, the easy rivers, like the Gila and the Salt, the San Juan, the Green, the upper Colorado and others were those that would see the earliest viable development. The lower Colorado was just far too much trouble to fool with. After all, a good part of it lay buried in a mile deep canyon that only the Indians and a few crazy white men had ever seen and precious little of the rest of it could even be accessed without grueling, months-long overland expeditions. Any attempts to use the lower river's waters for agricultural purposes by digging canals and lateral ditches were wiped out on a fairly regular basis by raging spring floods. All in all, it was a hard river to love. And in many respects, there's not a great deal of difference today; no major metropolitan area sits along its banks, access roads are relatively few, nine-tenths of it are cliff-bound and more than a thousand of its 1,450-mile length runs through deep canyons.

Since 400 A.D. various groups of Indians have lived in the canyons of the Colorado and attempted to live in harmony with the river and eke out a living along its banks and the canyon walls. The last of those, the "Anasazi," gave up the struggle and left the area somewhere in the time span of the 1300s. Following that exodus, it was not until approximately 1540 when Spanish explorations touched briefly on rim top overlook observations that concluded there was little there to merit further exploratory investigation. It took a one-armed Civil War veteran to finally unlock the mysteries the river's canyon held so closely, some three hundred years after the Spaniards gave up on the notion.

Major John Wesley Powell set out from Green River, Wyoming on May 24, 1869 with nine men and four boats on a mission to travel the river from there to the confluence of the Colorado and Virgin Rivers in Southern Nevada. Thirteen weeks later with six remaining men and only two boats, he emerged from the Grand Canyon, hungry, exhausted, and physically diminished. But he had an amazing tale to tell. Yet even that amazing accomplishment was not enough. Undaunted by the hardships he suffered on that first marvelous adventure, he repeated the feat a second time in 1871 in order to flesh out the details and provide a better scientific explanation of the river's geological story.

Those who have been fortunate enough to experience the river through the Grand Canyon will readily understand that to state simply that John Wesley Powell was an amazing man is an understatement in the extreme. To duplicate his adventures on the river with today's sophistication in boats and equipment represents challenge aplenty for the sound of body and young of heart. To consider such an undertaking with fragile wooden boats and a maimed body stuns the imagination.

The simple way to approach an understanding of the man's tenacity is to read his own words set down in a journal as he plunged into the abyss of America's last great unknown. Here is but a single excerpt that says as much about the man as one will ever need to know:

> "We start up a gulch; then pass to a bench along the wall; then up again over broken rock; then we reach more benches, along which we walk, until we find more broken rocks and crevices, by which we climb; still up, until we have ascended 600 or 800 feet, when we are met by a sheer precipice. Looking about, we find a place where it seems possible to climb. I go ahead; Bradley hands the barometer to me, and follows. So we proceed, stage by stage, until we are nearly at the summit. Here, by making a spring, I gain a foothold in a little crevice, and grasp an angle of the rock

overhead. I find that I can go up no farther and cannot step back, for I dare not let go with my hand and cannot reach foothold below without. I call to Bradley for help. He finds a way by which he can get to the top of the rock over my head, but cannot reach me. Then he looks around for some stick or limb of a tree, but finds none. Then he suggests that he would better help me with the barometer case, but I fear I cannot hold on to it. The moment is critical. Standing on my toes, my muscles begin to tremble. It is sixty or eighty feet to the foot of the precipice. If I lose my hold I shall fall to the bottom and then perhaps roll over the bench and tumble still farther down the cliff. At this instant it occurs to Bradley to take off his drawers, which he does, and swings them down to me. I hug close to the rock, let go with my hand, seize the dangling legs, and with his assistance am enabled to gain the top. Then we walk out on the peninsular rock, make the necessary observations for determining its altitude above camp, and return, finding an easy way down."
From: Exploration of the Colorado River of The West And its Canyons, by John Wesley Powell.

Major Powell wrote that as though death defying, one-armed cliff hanging events were the everyday norm to be expected as part of the job. At the time of his first exploration, Powell mistakenly believed the Green River, heading in Wyoming's Wind River Range, was the Colorado River's main stem and the then-called, Grand River, was a tributary. The reverse is of course true, but given the greater length of the Green River and denied the sophistication of modern satellite mapping capabilities he can easily be forgiven his error. But in all other aspects of his analysis, Major Powell was correct, and most particularly in his optimistic forecasts of the river system's ability to open and support development of the Great Southwest of the United States on a massive scale.

John Wesley Powell's second voyage, 1871.
J. W. Powell's "Arid Lands" report photo.

Soon after Powell's second exploration of the river in 1871, serious farming ventures along the lower Colorado River's east bank at its confluence with the Gila River began to take hold near present day Yuma, AZ. A child of the Civil War, the Arizona Territory was adding adventurous souls to its population at an astounding rate. Foodstuffs shipped from California could not keep up with demand and that obvious state of affairs spurred a booming agricultural economy wherever there was water enough to support it.

The Salt River Valley, site of present day Phoenix, was one such important agricultural area. The Yuma-Mohawk-Welton areas along the lower Gila and the Colorado were others. On the California side of the Colorado, visionary entrepreneurs began to eye a silt-rich valley that was a freak of geological history as a potential agricultural pot of gold. The "Salton Sink," as it was then known, was a 2100-square mile basin with a floor that varied between 180 and 225 feet below sea level and was blessed with incredibly fertile soils.

In prehistoric times the Colorado was a wild, raging, monstrous river that carried silt loads that defy imagination or description. With such huge quantities of material to work with the river created an enormous thirty mile long natural levee at its mouth that effectively divided the Gulf of California in half on a northeast-southwest diagonal. On a whim, as was its habit, the river eventually began to flow along the southeastern side of the levee it had built, creating a salt water lake on the northwestern side in the bargain. Over time, measured in centuries, that salt-water lake evaporated and the result was the creation of the aforementioned "Salton Sink."

Time after time the river toyed with the Sink over the ages like it was a plaything, alternately flooding it with a silt and nutrient-laden fresh water lake, then abandoning it once again to be left to evaporate completely away. The result was a plain of virtually rock-free incredibly rich, fertile soil that required no preparation or amendment before planting.

For promotional purposes, developers grandly proclaimed the place to be the "Imperial Valley," as they constructed irrigation canals and laterals to carry the river's life giving water to this incredible inland oasis. The California Development Company promised uninterrupted year-round growing seasons, limitless irrigation water, spectacular soil fertility, and sky-is-the-limit economic prosperity to farmers willing to buy into this can't-miss utopia.

And buy in they did, establishing fantastic farms, orchards, and vineyards to grow barley, alfalfa, cotton, table grapes, melons, citrus fruits, vegetables of all varieties and other oil-seed crops. The "Imperial Valley" turned out to be everything developers promised and then some. And with the coming of the railroads there seemed to be no end to the bonanza. In 1877 the Southern Pacific railroad bridge across the Colorado River at Yuma was completed and Southern California farm crops could now access markets across the length and breadth of the nation. A new era of prosperity was ushered in as another faded away. Steamboat traffic along the Colorado River was now relegated to the historical archives as a quaint relic of the past.

A Colorado River steamboat.
Salt River Project/Arizona Historical Society photo.

But as though resentful and petulant at being taken for granted and ignored, the mighty Colorado displayed its precocious character in February of 1905, when it switched paths, as it had so many times throughout geological history. It surged along the accommodating canals the California Development Company had created for it, to inundate scores of farms and orchards in the Imperial Valley. The livelihood of hundreds was at stake as the river reclaimed tract after tract. It was immediately apparent to all that the entire Imperial Valley was at high risk if the river was left unchecked.

And with this act of natural defiance, the Colorado River effectively sealed its fate. This sort of behavior could not be tolerated and so, humankind was left without options and war was declared on the river. If man was to live in peaceful coexistence with the Colorado River, it must first be tamed and controlled. Who would be master? Mankind or the river—there could be but one.

The California Development Company and the valley farmers turned to the Southern Pacific Railroad's president, E. H. Harriman, for help in the battle against the unruly river. This was a problem much bigger than a few men with sandbags and shovels could hope to deal with, and the Southern Pacific had a vested interest in the Imperial Valley's continued success and prosperity.

Harriman rolled up his sleeves and attacked the problem with gusto, marshalling the best and the brightest of S.P.'s engineers and construction crews and assembling an armada of railroad rolling stock and excavating equipment. But it would require nearly two years of dogged determination before Harriman's small army could set the river right again and force it back into its proper channel.

Tons of rock and earth fill, together with pile and timber dams, and even sandbags numbered in the tens of thousands, had been employed in the battle to steer the chocolate colored waters away from the valley's canal system. And at long last, victory in that first battle was declared on November 4, 1906 while the river flow was at its seasonal low.

Floodwaters began to percolate into the soil and evaporate away, but celebrations were short lived. Scarcely a month later the river broke free again, sweeping away man's feeble attempts at restraint as though they never existed and cutting a gash through the earthworks over 1,000 feet long and as much as 40 feet deep in places.

Harriman understood that if lasting solutions to the river's mischief were to be obtained it would require a Herculean effort far beyond what his crews had accomplished thus far. With government encouragement and cooperation he devised a bold plan to stop the river's invasion of the Imperial Valley once and for all. He proposed a pair of trestles to be constructed over the length of the river's latest spillway that would allow side-dump rail cars to discharge earth and rock fill directly into the gap at a rate faster than the river could carry it away. His engineers reckoned it could be done but it would take not less than 1,000 such cars operating round-the-clock for as long as two weeks or more to stop the river, once the trestles were in place.

And therein was the nut. Dumping the fill faster than the river could wash it away was simply a matter of mathematics. Building trestles over 1,000 feet long across a river flow on a silty bottom faster than the river could carry THOSE away was another matter. Harriman was undeterred. Throw enough men, money, and equipment at any task and a man could accomplish anything he set his mind to. After all, it was only a river. If you could build railroads across hostile deserts from Los Angeles to El Paso and beyond, taming a river's spillover should be child's play. "Stop it at all costs," he commanded.

But the Colorado River would not suffer defeat easily. Three times it tore trestle construction apart and sent timbered members spinning on the current. But then, finally, a single span was completed and Harriman quickly set the plan in motion while the structure still stood and before the river could tear it asunder.

For 15 consecutive days, train after train backed dump cars onto the spindle-trestle to discharge tens of thousands of cubic yards of rocky fill into the gap. And on February 10, 1907, the cut was closed off and the river returned to its original channel. The Imperial Valley had been saved.

Remnant evidence of this bit of calamitous river history still exists today in the form of the "Salton Sea," a shallow inland lake east of Indio, California, that includes a national recreation area.

Three years and three million dollars later, man had won another battle with the river, but it was abundantly clear to all concerned that the victory was a temporary one and the war against the river was not yet decided. Another huge spring surge could come in any year and send the river on another devastating rampage.

To the east, farmers of the Arizona Territory's Salt River Valley had already experienced big problems with an unruly river. A decade before the Colorado River's Imperial Valley flood, the Salt River overflowed its banks with catastrophic result, nearly wiping out the young community of Phoenix.

The Salt River flood took place in February 1891: unusual in that it was in the dead of winter and not a springtime runoff surge. The river spread to a width of as much as eight miles in places and wrought enormous damage. Much of what is today's downtown high-rise commercial core in Phoenix would be under water were a similar flood to take place now. The approaches to the railroad bridge over the Salt at Tempe were washed out to leave Phoenix without rail service and therefore physically isolated for months. If the river could do this much damage in winter, what was it capable of in a springtime following a big mountain snow pack?

Salt River flooding. Salt River Project/Arizona Historical Society photo.

As an interesting sidebar for those interested in such things, this was the flood that proved to be the undoing of Jacob Waltz of "Lost Dutchman Mine" fame. The flood inundated his small farm and house and he was forced to spend a bone-chilling winter night, soaked through and shivering, clinging to a tree. He died from pneumonia shortly thereafter, taking the secrets of his mine's location to the grave with him. If that were the extent of the flood's consequences, most would have been relieved. But after the flood's devastation was repaired the region immediately came under scorching drought conditions.

The Salt River then became little more than a trickle, its level inadequate to serve much of the irrigation canal systems that had been developed. Accounts of the time tell us that not less than a third of the farmlands under cultivation in the 1890s failed completely, riverside wells dried up, orchards were transformed into forests of firewood, livestock perished, and families by the score packed up and left the place, convinced Phoenix was doomed.

And as if all of that were not enough, the 1890s drought ended in yet another flood that wiped away the irrigation diversion dams to allow hundreds of thousands of acre-feet of precious water to run away to the Gulf, completely wasted.

Salt River flooding. Salt River Project/Arizona Historical Society photo.

All of this relates to the California experience with the Colorado River floods in this manner; it was the Salt River calamities in Arizona that led to the passage of the "Newlands Reclamation Act" of 1902. Within the act was the authorization to organize the "U.S. Reclamation Service," the forerunner of today's Bureau of Reclamation, and, the authorization for federal funding of low-cost loans for western irrigation projects, and by extension, flood control works.

Californians looking for flood control measures further benefited by observations of the Arizona experience with what sort of obstacles must first be cleared before federal money could be obtained. Federal loans would require repayment, with the terms of said repayment clearly set forth in a written contract. But a contractual agreement requires at least two parties. If the Federal Government was prepared to lend money, someone or some entity, must be available to receive it, and, to guarantee repayment by execution of the contract.

While that may sound like a reasonable and logical, if not fundamental, requirement, arriving at a consensus of opinion as to whom the responsible Salt River party would be was quite another matter. The question of water rights would have to be addressed first and foremost. Several canal companies were in operation and the developing founders quickly insisted they should be the responsible parties with exclusive rights regarding ownership and distribution of any water that resulted from new irrigation projects. The farmers, who would actually be the end users of the water, obviously believed otherwise.

In Washington meanwhile, President Theodore Roosevelt chafed at the bickering between Arizona factions that stood squarely in the way of any real progress on the ground and threatened to withdraw any offers of federal involvement or assistance if the opposing parties could not resolve their differences.

The desperate need for a large storage and flood control impoundment somewhere upstream had been obvious to all concerned for a number of years. A dam site selection committee had been formed as early as 1889 to find the best location for such an installation, and an ideal site at the confluence of Tonto Creek and the Salt River had already been selected. Everything was in place to solve the problem and break the continuous flood-drought cycle once and for all: the money, the will, and the proper topography. Only the legal issues remained to be resolved.

Judge Joseph H. Kibbey, presiding over the Territorial equivalent of a State Superior Court and who would later go on to become Governor, cracked the nut by rendering a definitive decision describing water rights on the basis of "prior appropriation" borrowed from old Spanish law. In essence, the "Kibbey Decision," which remains at the foundation of modern Arizona water law, held that the water belongs to the LAND where it was first put to beneficial use. The water did not belong to the canal companies to sell. They could only sell the distribution service. Not the product itself.

With that matter finally resolved, the way was cleared for the July, 1903 establishment of the "Salt River Valley Water Users Association," the legal entity with which the Federal Government could now enter into contractual agreement with. Some 4,000-valley landowners signed on as members of the association, pledging 200,000 acres of fee-simple lands as security for a federal loan.

Each pledged acre represented a single share of stock in the association and John P. Orme was elected Association President with authority to execute contracts on the association's behalf. Things then began to move rapidly. By October 1903, an engineer of the U.S. Reclamation Service arrived in Phoenix to begin plans for the construction of what would be the world's highest dam, and the first project undertaken by the fledgling service. To the west, Californians watched the unfolding events in Arizona carefully and with great interest. There was much to be learned and taken as valuable lessons from the Arizona example.

The dam planned to harness Arizona's Salt River was ambitious in the extreme when the era and the then current state of technological sophistication is considered. In 1905 the world ran on steam power and horse muscle. Development of the internal combustion engine was still in its infancy and the gargantuan wheeled and tracked earth moving equipment we are accustomed to today was not yet even dreamed of. Aside from steam-powered dragline shovels, the principal digging tools were hammer and hand drill, dynamite, picks, spades, and a good man's back.

The properties and sophistication of reinforced concrete construction were not quite there yet either. In the early 20th Century, if you wanted to build big, you built with quarry stone, not concrete. And so, Roosevelt Dam, as it would come to be called in honor of our 26th President, would be an arched dam constructed of native stone 284 feet high, 170 feet thick at the base, tapering to 16 feet wide at the top, and spanning over 1,000 feet from canyon wall to canyon wall.

Italian stonecutters were brought in to quarry the stone blocks directly from the canyon walls near the construction site, with the first such stone laid in 1906. Just five years later, on February 5, 1911, the dam was completed. On March 18, 1911, former President Theodore Roosevelt dedicated it. That pace of construction was quite amazing when one considers that the construction site was a five-day horse ride from Phoenix over primitive trails and the military wagon roads of the time. And when you arrived at the site, there was *NOTHING THERE.*

Before dam construction could even begin, a town would first have to be built in order to accommodate the work force and the families, complete with churches, eateries, a post office, a bank, general store, schools and all else that goes together to make a complete functioning community. Oddly, for an Arizona town of the times though, there would be no bawdy houses, saloons, or gambling establishments, much to the delight and approval of the entrepreneurs of Globe City, a two-day ride to the south.

But much more than a town would be needed. A small dam and hydroelectric plant was built and installed 20 miles upstream from the primary dam site in order to provide electrical power to the new town and to the dam's construction site. A cement mill to convert native lime and clay deposits into Portland cement was built above the new town. Telephone and telegraph lines from Phoenix to Globe City and thence to the new town of "Roosevelt" were installed. Practical roads to accommodate heavy wagon traffic were built to negotiate steep canyons, professional hunters were employed and dispatched to provide fresh meat for the labor force, farm plots were prepared to provide produce, and an ice plant was built to preserve it all.

All of this had to be done before the first foundation stone could be laid in place. But this amazing accomplishment gave proof that man could tame any western river under any circumstances if he set his mind to it. Roosevelt Dam was essentially built by hand in a deep, rocky, inaccessible canyon in the wild Arizona interior in just five years at a cost of ten million 1906 dollars. And as the years would pass, the Salt River Project would repay the entire construction debt owed the Federal Government by 1955, through the sale of hydro-generated electricity.

Italian stonecutters at Roosevelt Dam.
Salt River Project/Arizona Historical Society photo.

Work in progress at Roosevelt Dam.
Salt River Project/Arizona Historical Society photo.

Work in Progress at Roosevelt Dam.
Salt River Project/Arizona Historical Society photo.

*The completed project. Salt River Project/Arizona
Historical Society photo.*

Other downstream dams in the Salt River system would be added in time, but it was Roosevelt Dam that set the example for what could be done to put the mighty Colorado River under man's control and the lessons were not lost on the farmers who remained at that great river's mercy.

With the Arizona example and the Salton Sea calamity firmly in mind, Reclamation engineers went to work on a series of practical on-the-ground investigations of what might be possible and what was not in the quest to control the Colorado River. In short order they discovered the need to think in terms of far greater scale than the Salt River's project had been. Their studies involved more than 1,000 miles of river and as many as 70 possible dam sites.

But planning on such a scale was not an overnight proposition. Years dragged on as the world fought the war to end all wars and dealt with the Spanish Flu pandemic at the same time. These were matters of far greater importance than flood control and irrigation projects in America's far flung west. Consequently, reclamation projects simmered on the back burner until late in 1918 when Reclamation Commissioner and Chief Engineer, Arthur P. Davis, advanced a radical proposal.

Davis insisted that the success of the Salt River's Roosevelt Dam could be duplicated or exceeded with a similar high dam on the Colorado River if it were to be properly sited. That is, in a deep canyon choke point at the foot of an adequate storage basin, again, much like the Roosevelt Dam and lake example. But the location he advocated met the desired criteria on a scale of staggering proportion.

Davis's proposed dam site was in Black Canyon, a few miles south of Las Vegas on the Colorado River between Nevada and Arizona. The envisioned dam itself, to be constructed of concrete, would surpass Roosevelt Dam in height and design to impound the largest manmade lake in the United States.

Before a project of such scope could be entertained however, the matter of water rights would have to be addressed, as was the case, once again, citing the Arizona experience. But while rights to an interior river's water involving a few thousand farmers was one thing, water rights to the Colorado would ultimately involve seven states and a foreign country.

Two years would pass before the Davis proposal gained enough traction, attention, and support to prompt the governors of the Colorado River Basin states to consider a meeting of their respective representatives to discuss and negotiate an agreement to determine how the river's waters might be equitably divided. In 1921, all seven states then appointed commissioners; by an act of Congress, the U.S. Secretary of Commerce, Herbert Hoover, was named as the Federal Representative to the proceedings.

The first objective of determining an equitable division of the river's water was immediately stalled because there was no common denominator between the various states for determining individual water rights. Arizona's first-in-time approach might work well enough for Arizona but other states had differing methods that were not compatible with the "prior appropriation" doctrine.

Colorado's representative to the proceedings, Delph E. Carpenter, then proposed a cut-to-the-chase solution that finally cleared the way toward a meeting of the minds. He suggested that instead of attempting to deal with and sort out the details of individual water rights within the states, which would obviously require adjudication and might consume decades before a resolution was obtained, a far better and less complicated approach would be to simply divide the entire drainage basin into two parts—an upper and a lower basin, with the river's water divided equally between those two basins.

Under Carpenter's plan, the states within each basin could then negotiate with each other at some future juncture, to determine who would receive what, and beyond that, an individual state involved could sort out the further subdivision of its share of the river to settle the matter of internal water rights exclusively. There was no need, clearly, for the State of Colorado, for example, to be concerned with individual water rights within the State of California.

His proposal put the dividing line between the upper and lower basins at Lees Ferry near the confluence of the Paria and Colorado Rivers. It further provided that the Colorado's water be apportioned between upper and lower basins at the rate of 7.5 million acre-feet annually for each, with the lower basin granted the right to increase its beneficial consumptive use of the water by one million acre-feet per water year.

Carpenter's proposal was adopted, agreed to, and ratified and signed by six of the seven basin state representatives in November 1922 in Santa Fe, New Mexico, to be thereinafter referred to as the 1922 Santa Fe Compact. The "Compact" did not provide for the allocation of water to any individual state. Its purpose was simply to cut through legal entanglements and create a larger framework within which the states could further negotiate among themselves. Nor did the Compact address the disposition or methods that might be necessarily employed in the event the Colorado's flow was inadequate to fulfill the agreement's mandated division of 15 million acre-feet of water in any given water year.

The six Colorado River Basin states that were signatory to the original 1922 Compact were California, Nevada, Utah, New Mexico, Wyoming, and Colorado. Arizona abstained and would not ratify and sign the Compact until 1944. Nonetheless, the 1922 Santa Fe Compact, flawed as it may have been, cleared the way for the Davis proposal to go forward to build a flood control dam and a storage impoundment on the Colorado River.

The next order of business then would be to further refine the purpose and function of such a project. How and by whom would the impoundment be used and administered, and to what and whose advantage? Although the proposed dam and resulting lake would be within the bordering states of Nevada and Arizona, these two states had no means of access or utilization of the impounded water. Downstream, only California, through its rudimentary and primitive diversion and canal systems could claim any current or historical beneficial diversionary use of the Colorado River waters.

These realities set the early stage for considerable disagreement among California, Arizona, and Nevada representatives regarding the equitable division of the lower basin's 7.5 – plus million acre foot annual share of the river water. Six more years of alternating floods and dry-ups would plague the lower basin farmers while negotiations continued to stumble along. Then finally, in 1928, Congress passed the "Boulder Canyon Project Act" over Arizona's objections. The law authorized the construction of the high dam in Black Canyon or Boulder Canyon that Davis had originally proposed, but beyond that it also authorized construction of the "All-American Canal" to tie the Imperial and Coachella Valleys of California with the Colorado River—all at an authorized expenditure of $165 million.

In March, 1931, the newly reorganized "Bureau of Reclamation" opened bidding for the construction of Hoover Dam and later awarded contracts to "Six Companies, Inc.," a conglomerate, with notice to proceed with the first step in the long-range development of the Colorado River.

Downstream some 150 miles from the Hoover Dam site, an equally important diversion structure would also be built under the Act. This would be the Parker Dam project, which would provide additional water metering regulation, power generation, and a de-silting catchment for the 240-mile long "Colorado River Aqueduct," a canal system that would deliver water to San Diego and Los Angeles.

Arizona, as the lone holdout in the 1922 Compact ratification, objected to all of this because no provisions for defining Arizona's share of the river, if any, had yet to be firmly established. Under the "Swing-Johnson Bill," which was the basis for the Boulder Canyon Project Act, an implied apportionment had been "suggested" that would provide 4.4 million acre-feet of water to California annually, while Arizona was to be guaranteed 2.8 million acre-feet, with 300,00 acre-feet apportioned to Nevada, with the further provision that Arizona and California could split any surplus above the 7.5 million acre-foot per water-year guarantee. It was, however, only a suggestion, and was not set forth as a guaranteed provision in the law's final, approved version.

Consequently, Arizona asked the U.S. Supreme Court to block construction of Hoover Dam and related infrastructure until the issue of guaranteed apportionment could be resolved. The Court however rejected Arizona's argument and upheld the Constitutionality of the Swing-Johnson Bill in 1931, removing any legal obstacle to the Hoover Dam project. Conquest of the Colorado River was nearing realization at long last. Once all legal blocks were removed, work at Hoover Dam progressed at a rapid pace despite the need to overcome huge topographical and logistic obstacles similar to those encountered with Roosevelt Dam's construction. Water storage began in February 1935, and President Franklin D. Roosevelt dedicated the essentially completed dam in September. The first generator went on-line and began producing power in October 1936.

Downstream, Parker Dam, impounding 45-mile long Lake Havasu, was completed two years later, though not without controversy and much to the displeasure of Arizona's Governor and Legislature who had fought tooth and nail to scuttle the entire project.

At issue for Arizona, as always, was the now well established means of water distribution to Southern California while Arizona had to be content with literally dipping buckets and doing so without legal authority at that. If there were any doubts regarding Arizona's resolve in the matter, they should have been put to rest by Arizona Governor, Ben Moer's actions, in March 1934. When engineers, workers, and equipment appeared on the California side of the river to begin work on Parker Dam, Moer dispatched a National Guard unit to patrol the dam site in a pair of obsolete steam-powered river boats.

The boats, the *Julia B.* and the *Nellie T.,* promptly became hopelessly entangled in steel cables and the crews of both, forever enshrined by the newspapers of the period as the "Desert Sailors," had to be rescued by the "enemy Californians."

The inglorious defeat of Arizona's Navy and its battleships did not however deter or end Governor Moer's crusade. In November he sent a National Guard infantry Company, complete with 20 machinegun crews, to guard the "front" against construction of a trestle bridge that was necessary to the dam's construction, and without which, work could not proceed.

Fortunately, no shots were fired and no one was hurt as work ground to a halt while the Interior Department asked the U.S. Supreme Court for an injunction. It was of course granted, and Arizona was then under court order not to interfere with the dam's construction. Arizona complied, but would not allow workers to establish temporary living quarters on the Arizona side, nor could fuel or other supplies necessary to support construction be purchased in Arizona.

Planning for yet another Colorado River dam began in 1938. This one would be located in "Pyramid Canyon," between Parker and Hoover Dams. Construction of Davis Dam was authorized in 1941, but with the outbreak of World War II and the need to husband critical construction materials for the war effort, progress came to a standstill. It would be 1946 before construction at Davis Dam could resume.

That project, completed in 1952 at a cost of $65 million, together with the added downstream distribution and metering facilities at Imperial, Headgate Rock, Palo Verde, Laguna, and Morelos Dams, permitted treaty obligations with Mexico to be met.

Davis Dam, impounding Lake Mohave, was combined with Parker Dam to form the Parker-Davis Unit for efficiency purposes. When combined with Hoover Dam, the power output of the three dams is enormous, providing a power pool that serves much of the industrial, agricultural, and residential needs of a large part of Southern California, Arizona, and Southern Nevada.

Hoover Dam site.
Department of the Interior/Bureau of Reclamation photo.

Hoover Dam construction.
Department of the Interior/Bureau of Reclamation photo.

Hoover Dam construction.
Department of the Interior/Bureau of Reclamation photo.

Hoover Dam completed.
Department of the Interior/Bureau of Reclamation photo.

The lower river was now completely controlled, much to the delight of southern Californians, who need not fear catastrophic flooding or devastating drought conditions ever again. But Arizona and Nevada were still shut out of the lower basin water-sharing picture with no resolution on the horizon. It is not difficult to understand why. There was no incentive whatsoever for California to agree to open water-sharing negotiations with her sister states. Any such formal agreement produced by negotiations would obviously result in LESS water for California—not more.

The upper basin states, on the other hand, came together in 1948 to discuss an equitable water-sharing plan among them. An interesting wrinkle in the geographical demarcation line between the upper and lower basins was that Arizona was the only one of the seven basin states that had a legitimate claim to BOTH upper and lower basins. This resulted from a small slice of the northeast corner of Arizona providing a marginal part of the San Juan River's drainage basin. As a result, the apportionment agreement that came of the "Upper Basin Compact" provided an annual 50,000 acre/foot allotment to Arizona. Of the remaining 7.5 million acre/feet reserved to the upper basin,

51.75% was allocated to Colorado, 23% to Utah, 14% to Wyoming, and 11.25% to New Mexico.

The cooperation among the upper basin states in arriving at a swift water sharing agreement paved the way for development planning. Enormous effort and untold millions of dollars had been dedicated to development improvements of the lower river for the benefit of California and Mexico, but nothing had yet been done to make it possible for any upper basin state to withdraw any significant quantity of the river's waters that were allotted to them.

By treaty, Mexico was guaranteed 1.5 million acre/feet per year. Aside from that established obligation, there was nothing to prevent California from using all that remained of the lower basin's guaranteed 7.5 million acre/feet as well; in addition with, for that matter, all of the upper basin's allotted water, since there existed no means for the upper basin states to capture their water. A network of dams in the upper basin, similar to those already in place downstream, would be required in order to do so.

Planning for the network of upper basin dams that would be needed commenced immediately with the key to the entire system founded in the one great dam that was proposed at the foot of "Glen Canyon," just fifteen miles upstream from Lees Ferry in northern Arizona. With this dam in place, the upper basin states would at last have a practical means of metering the 7.5 million acre/feet per year downstream allotment obligation established in the 1922 Santa Fe Compact.

Diversion facilities and release metering dams on several of the Colorado River tributaries such as Flaming Gorge, Blue Mesa, Navajo, and other dams, were planned in connection with Glen Canyon Dam to provide a practical working water system for upper basin beneficial use. Meanwhile, the dispute between Arizona and California over river water raged on, and was eventually left to the U.S. Supreme Court to settle. The apportionment suggested decades earlier by the "Swing-Johnson Bill" was apparently not enough to satisfy California. Under Swing-Johnson, California was to be guaranteed 4.4 million acre/feet per year, but California insisted it should be entitled to 5.36 million acre/feet, arguing that a million acre feet of Gila River water, which was tributary to the Colorado, should be counted as part of Arizona's share of Colorado River water.

California's position was complicated by prior appropriation rights to Gila River water claims by New Mexico, as well as Arizona's adjudicated Salt River water rights, which were tributary to the Gila. Moreover, Arizona lawyers argued that the Gila River, whose total water rights were still subject to an ongoing adjudication process that was likely to prove that river was indeed over-subscribed, entered the Colorado River just a few miles above the international border without effect to California.

In any event, the Supreme Court rejected California's argument and ruled that California's share was to be fixed at 4.4 million acre/feet, Arizona's at 2.8 million acre/feet, and Nevada's at 300,000 acre/feet, all as originally set forth in "Swing-Johnson."

The Supreme Court decision determining once and for all how the lower basin allotment would be divided was not handed down until 1963, the same year, by coincidence, that the Glen Canyon Dam project would be completed. In so doing, the court cleared the way for authorization of the Central Arizona Project. The U.S. Senate had twice before approved the "CAP," but the U.S. House Interior Committee would not pass out a bill until Arizona was able to prove that it had a legal entitlement to Colorado River water. The Supreme Court ruling established that, but it would not be until 1968 when the "CAP Bill" was passed and sent to President Lyndon Johnson to be signed into law.

Similar in scope to the California Aqueduct and the All-American Canal, the CAP would consist of a canal system that would draw water from Lake Havasu at Parker Dam and deliver it to the Phoenix and Tucson metro areas as well as agricultural entities along the way.

Like the first project of The Department of Reclamation on Arizona's Salt River, work at Glen Canyon Dam would require living quarters for a work force and their families, roads, and supporting infrastructure installations before any significant work at the river's dam site could begin. But while situated in one of the most desolate and remote regions of the United States, these initial requirements would not be easily met. Vertical canyon walls that rose seven hundred feet or more above the river enclosed the proposed dam site. Before a cableway and footbridge would be installed, it took most of a day to drive an automobile from one canyon rim to the other and the only possible means of reaching the site on the river was by boat.

A temporary crew camp was established on the west side of the canyon in 1956 as preliminary work at the site commenced. Before a similar and permanent base of operations could be located on the east side, however, a land trade would first be required because all of that terrain was Navajo Nation tribal land. With a trade involving as much as 24 square miles in the works, "Government Camp" was then established on the east side atop a plateau called Manson Mesa.

Government Camp would go on in later years to evolve into the Incorporated Community of Page, but in 1956 and '57 it consisted of a smattering of tin-side trailers with only the very basic and rudimentary necessities of life.

In October 1956, President Eisenhower pushed a button in Washington, D.C., far across the country, that triggered the first dynamite blast at the Glen Canyon site to signal the beginning of work at the project, but it was largely a ceremonial event. There could be no real progress until the canyon was bridged so workers could cross from one side to the other, and until a cableway could be installed to allow equipment to be lowered and raised to and from the riverbed.

The post-tensioned steel cable footbridge that was first installed tested the courage of all who were obliged to use it. Five feet wide and a thousand feet long and supported by a high-tension system of cables that sang an eerie song whenever the wind blew, the best advice given to first-time crossers was to look straight ahead and just put one foot in front of the other.

Much the same could be said of the "birdcage" on the cableway that soon followed. The birdcage was the moniker given the cross-canyon cable tram that later transported workers to and fro, some 800 feet above the river and made construction of the high-arch bridge possible.

Perry Olmstead, a carpenter who would spend seven years of his life working on the Glen Canyon Dam project had this to say about riding the birdcage:

"I had to cross the canyon on it three times before I screwed up enough courage to open my eyes, and then I wished I hadn't! The High Scalers didn't think nothing about it. But of course Merritt-Chapman paid them boys four-eighty an hour to be fearless. And that was back before the strike. I was making a dollar less than that so I had ever right to be a coward."

Construction of the high-arch bridge that would carry vehicle traffic and is today familiar to all who travel Highway 89 across the canyon began in May 1957 and was completed and open to traffic in February 1959. With both the vehicle-capable bridge and a heavy-lift cableway in place, serious work on the dam itself could now go forward.

Glen Canyon Bridge site, 1958.
Department of the Interior/Bureau of Reclamation photo.

Bridge under construction.
Department of the Interior/Bureau of Reclamation photo.

Bridge under construction.
Department of the Interior/Bureau of Reclamation photo.

Bridge completed in 1959.
Department of the Interior/Bureau of Reclamation photo.

GLEN CANYON BRIDGE
700 FEET ABOVE THE COLORADO
RIVER
THE HIGHEST STEEL ARCH BRIDGE
IN THE WORLD
LENGTH OF ARCH....1028' ROADWAY WIDTH....30'
LENGTH OF DECK....1271' WORK STARTED MAY 1957
VERTICAL RISE OF ARCH 165' COMPLETED FEB....1959

Bridge details, 1960
Department of the Interior/Bureau of Reclamation photo.

Bird's eye view of Glen Canyon Dam site, 1959.
Department of the Interior/Bureau of Reclamation photo.

And go forward it did, achieving award winning engineering records of accomplishment over the course of its seven year construction period. The statistics associated with the dam's construction produce mind-numbing data bits in size and scope that are difficult to comprehend. Consider the raw numbers: from bedrock to crest the dam is 710 feet high and rises 587 feet above the river itself. It is 1,560 feet long and 25 feet wide at the crest. The base is 300 feet wide, and the dam contains nearly five million cubic yards of concrete. Its eight powerhouse turbines have a generating capacity of 1,296,000 kilowatts.

To help put such numbers into perspective, try visualizing them in football field terms. Seven hundred and ten feet is roughly equal to two football fields plus decent field-goal range, and the crest length is equal to FIVE football fields plus a field goal. What about almost 1.3 million kilowatts? How does one put that into perspective? It might help to understand that it is enough to power over a half-million households. Multiply that by 2.5 occupants and you arrive at a million and a quarter people.

The lake that Glen Canyon Dam impounds, Lake Powell, is the second largest man-made lake in the United States, junior only to Lake Mead, its downstream cousin. Lake Powell extends some 180 miles upriver, with approximately 1,900 miles of shoreline and provides a storage capacity of 24 million acre-feet of water. Once again, the numbers are beyond easy grasp. How far is 1,900 miles? That's the approximate over-the-road distance between Salt Lake City and Toronto, Canada. And 24 million-acre feet is enough to put the entire State of Indiana under one foot of water.

In addition to its primary function as a water storage and metering tool, the lake, much as the case with its downstream sister impoundments, has proven itself to be a fantastic recreational destination that draws millions of visitors each year. Concessionaires provide marina services, lodging, tours, and watercraft rentals to cater to the recreational user's every practical wish.

The first of the concessionaires had his start in the river tour and guide service business long before any serious consideration had been given to the construction of Glen Canyon Dam. His name was Art Greene, and his connections to the Four Corners Region and the Colorado River ran deep. He had been providing river excursions to fabled Rainbow Bridge since the late 1940s and with the Dam's construction he simply picked up where he left off by establishing "Canyon Tours, Inc." as the first full-service concession on newly created Lake Powell.

Like David Rust who had pioneered guided river tours to Rainbow Bridge in the 1920s, Art Greene's early expeditions involved overland travel from his base of operations beneath northern Arizona's Vermillion Cliffs to Hite Crossing on the river below Cataract Canyon. There he inflated and launched war-surplus rubber boats for a down-river float to the junction of the river with Forbidding Canyon where an overland hike of several miles was required in order to visit the great stone arch. Following that, the float down-river continued for an additional five days before it reached the take-out point at Lees Ferry after numerous side-canyon explorations.

Later trips were accomplished with motorized boats that ran directly upriver to Rainbow Bridge from Lees Ferry, and still later, such boats evolved into a multi-passenger airboat that was utilized for a short time. Art christened the boat, *"Tseh Na-ni-ah-go Atin,"* a Navajo term that roughly translates to: "trail to rock that goes over." It was a name he would apply to other boats that would follow in years to come. But for the time being, the airboat so named, and of his own design and inspiration, was hugely popular with clients for its ability to skim over the river's shifting sand bars and provide an exhilarating ride. It eventually proved impractical for its fuel inefficiency and excessive noise, however, and Art was obliged to abandon it in favor of more conventional and fuel efficient designs.

Compared to the convenience and comfort of today's tour boat excursions, the pioneering river trips that Art Greene provided were somewhat austere. Participants were obliged to assist in angling for the river's catfish to supplement the evening meal that was prepared over an open campfire on the river's banks. But none complained too loudly after the visual impact of Rainbow Bridge had lodged itself in their conscience.

The world's largest natural stone bridge soars 291 feet high above, and 275 feet across. It lies in Bridge Canyon, a drainage that descends from 10,000-foot high Navajo Mountain on the Arizona-Utah border. But these numbers, like so many of those associated with Lake Powell or Glen Canyon Dam, are meaningless until one discovers this wonder in person and spends a quiet moment contemplating its majestic presence. Hard indeed is the heart that cannot be moved by this experience.

Rainbow Bridge is but one of numerous wonders tucked away in the seclusion of Glen Canyon, and Art Greene was determined to share as many of those as possible with a public that was largely oblivious to their existence. With Glen Canyon Dam's ability to begin capturing the river in 1963, his operations expanded rapidly with the establishment of Wahweap Lodge and Marina located on the west rim of Wahweap Canyon not far from the Dam, and operated by "Canyon Tours, Inc."

The Art Greene era came to a close in 1976 when the concession was sold to the Del Webb Corporation of Sun City fame, but not before Art Greene put Lake Powell on the recreational destination map and embedded it in the conscience of millions of Americans and world travelers.

A first step in the Dam's construction was the boring of twin bypass tunnels to allow the river's flow to continue unabated downstream while earth-fill coffer dams were erected at both upper and lower ends of the site. Those temporary dams permitted dry-up that enabled excavations to reach bedrock, and were engineering marvels in themselves, requiring hundreds of thousands of cubic yards of earth fill before the river could be effectively diverted.

Heavy equipment necessary at the site was lowered into place from the cross-canyon cableway, and larger pieces required teardown at the rims above, and reassembly once the item reached the canyon floor. Rail guided man-lift elevators were installed at the canyon walls to speed personnel to and from the work zones below. The guide rails were anchored to the rock walls by only the most determined effort by "High-Scalers," the men who did their work while dangling on an ordinary rope harness suspended from high above. Workers who rode the man-lift cars dubbed them "bird cages." A transit on one to the canyon floor was only slightly less terrifying than a cross-canyon commute on the cableway or the footbridge had been. Lifting winches and cables would jam from time to time, giving the "birdcage" occupants a jolt that brought a temporary halt to normal breathing.

Besides the constant danger associated with the work, living conditions for the 2,500-man work force and their families had only marginally improved at Government Camp on Manson Mesa by 1958. It was now called "Page," in honor of John C. Page, who had served as the Commissioner of the Bureau of Reclamation, and was now deceased. A few streets had been paved, but not enough to curb the dust and sand that flew through the air on a stiff breeze to dampen the spirits of wives left at home to attempt some degree of house keeping cleanliness. A handful of steel buildings had been erected to house schools and the few private businesses that opened on a dare by entrepreneurs inclined to bet on the income. A grocery store was housed in one of those steel buildings; the Babbitt Brothers Trading Company of Flagstaff and Northern Arizona opened it, but it was rarely fully stocked. More often than not, at least a third of the store's shelves were empty on any given day.

The store was supplied by a once-weekly truck delivery that made the four-hour haul from Flagstaff over a narrow two-lane road to carry the items of highest demand. If what was needed was not included in a shipment, Page residents were obliged to live without. Fresh meat and produce was most usually gone on the third day following a delivery. The same was true of newspapers and magazines, which represented the only source of news from the outside world besides almost non-existent AM radio broadcasts available late at night from far away cities.

According to Page resident of the period, Perry Olmstead, "I couldn't stay up too late at night because I needed to get out of bed pretty early in the morning. But I could get a laugh out of 'Wolf-Man Jack' at KOMA out of Oklahoma City if I could keep my eyes open 'till ten at night." That and a community dance, or perhaps a bingo game, or a 16mm film projected onto a white bed-sheet, was what passed for adult entertainment in the late 1950s at Page, Arizona.

The prime contractor, "Merritt, Chapman, and Scott," who had proved to be the low bidder on the project by as much as 10 million dollars under the next highest bidder, was having difficulties with its cost-accounting and was desperate to find cost-cutting solutions. At the end of 1958 it announced that it would no longer pay the six dollars per day subsistence bonus that had been intended to offset the living costs and difficulties workers had to endure at the remote job-site location.

The published rationale for this decision was that since the town of Page was now more or less self-sufficient, the daily subsistence pay was no longer justified. Not surprisingly, the workers disagreed, and a general strike was called that shut the entire project down on July 1, 1959. The strike lasted for six full months and during the interim period, Page became a virtual ghost town as many of the workers moved on to find jobs elsewhere. It was a difficult time and many of the entrepreneurs who had gambled on the future of Page were wiped out and forced to shutter their fledgling businesses. But the issues were eventually resolved and work on the project resumed early in 1960.

By June of that year, dignitaries and company officials gathered at the site to witness the first concrete pour from a giant, 24-ton capacity bucket. Once started, the process of placing concrete could not be interrupted. A previous pour could not be allowed to fully cure before the next could be placed atop it in order to maintain adhesion and avoid dry-joint faulting. Consequently, the concrete placement phase of construction continued, non-stop, day and night for three years.

Supporting this operation, the concrete batch-plant that operated 24-hours a day on the west canyon rim was the largest such operation in the United States at the time.

First concrete pour, 1960.
Department of the Interior/Bureau of Reclamation photo.

Concrete placement, 1961.
Department of the Interior/Bureau of Reclamation photo.

Glen Canyon Dam construction, 1961.
Department of the Interior/Bureau of Reclamation photo.

More than 400,000 24-ton buckets of concrete would be installed over a three-year period in order to complete the Dam. In all, the 5-million cubic yards of concrete utilized in the Dam's construction was enough to build a six-inch thick, four-lane highway from Phoenix, Arizona to Chicago, Illinois.

The bypass tunnels were closed in March 1963 to allow Lake Powell to begin filling. Installation of the turbines and power plant equipment followed and was completed in 1966. Lady Bird Johnson conducted the dedication ceremonies in September of that year, and the project was officially considered complete.

Contrary to popular legend, no workers were entombed in the Dam's concrete, although, sadly, seventeen men lost their lives over the course of the project's construction. And while that number was considerably less than the toll of lives required to build Hoover Dam, it was still far too many.

Glen Canyon Dam completed and Lake Powell filling.
Department of the Interior/Bureau of Reclamation photo.

Below Glen Canyon Dam, 1975. P. Klocki photo.

With the completion of Glen Canyon Dam, Lake Powell filled to "full-pool" capacity in 1980 to create a water wonderland accessible to millions of visitors annually. And as the lake expanded, so too did the city of Page, which incorporated in 1975 to become a modern, full-service American community of some 9,000 people. Its residents knew their city had come of age when a McDonalds franchise opened, and it had "arrived" when Wal-Mart built one of its big-box stores there.

Glen Canyon Dam, together with the later completed impoundments at Flaming Gorge, Navajo, and Blue Mesa Dams, and with numerous smaller diversion facilities, completed the Upper Colorado River Project. The upper basin states were now able to manage water requirements to realize their full growth potential. No longer were they helpless and obliged to stand by while watching their share of the Colorado River's waters disappear downstream for the benefit of others.

The entire upper basin storage system project, and most certainly the keystone feature, Glen Canyon Dam, was not without its detractors and considerable controversy that persists yet today. Within days of Glen Canyon Dam's completion, Bureau of Reclamation officials released the news that two more dams were in the planning stage for the Colorado River Project. One of the proposed dam sites was to be located in Marble Canyon, not far below Lees Ferry, and the other was planned for a site far down river in the Grand Canyon proper, at a place known as Bridge Canyon.

At the time, the "Sierra Club," an environmental advocacy organization of approximately 7,000 members, had been the chief antagonist of Reclamation's development plans for the Colorado River. That organization withdrew opposition to Glen Canyon Dam when agreement was reached to eliminate certain additional upstream facilities. When plans for the new downstream dams were announced, however, opposition to the building of ANY new dams on the river reached fever pitch.

Since then, the Dam has remained a celebrity cause for not just the Sierra Club, but also for any number of additional minor environmental fringe groups. In 1975, writer Edward Abbey released a novel entitled "The Monkey Wrench Gang," that claimed the Dam had ruined the river for all time. Some would argue that Glen Canyon Dam and Ed Abbey's book might have been the best things that ever happened to the Sierra Club; since 1963 that organization's membership has grown to more than 70,000 contributors, and without the Dam, numerous other smaller groups would have little justification for their existence.

Organizations such as the "Glen Canyon Institute" and others still call for the decommissioning of Glen Canyon Dam and the draining of Lake Powell. But such positions ignore today's realities and the concept of "the greater good." The realities are that Lake Powell's storage capacity exceeds that of all the other upper Colorado Project facilities combined and is the lynchpin of the entire distribution system. Without Glen Canyon Dam there would be no means for the upper basin states to regulate downstream release obligations. Moreover, without a multi-year storage reserve at Lake Powell, there would be no ability to provide water to the lower basin in times of extended drought. The value of this feature alone was ably demonstrated by the dry periods of 1989 through 1992 and more recently between 2000 and 2004 when, in both cases, Lake Powell was able to release full downstream allotment obligations regardless of below average inflow. Had Lake Powell not been in existence in 2004, Lake Mead would have become little more than a muddy puddle.

The argument that the Dam "ruined" the river makes the assumption that the river and Glen Canyon should have been preserved in a natural state. The question then arises, preserved for whom? And the presumptive answer would be, for those hale, hardy, and fit enough to visit the region by methods employed in the past; either by river boats of the Art Greene example, or by jeep, horse, or mule back.

In the days before Glen Canyon Dam was built, cumulative total visitation numbers for the river through the Glen Canyon environs are estimated to be less than 30,000 people. On a busy holiday weekend, it is not impossible for that many people to visit the area in a single day. Of those, very, very few leave Lake Powell disappointed by their experience. That is a fair example of service for the greater good.

More than 140 years after Major Powell's first observations of the Colorado River, his visions and prophesies of its future have been realized. Perhaps 1,000 years from now, the river will do the work that environmentalists demand by cutting through the dams and reclaiming an unfettered course to the sea. But for the moment, the Colorado River, a wild red river in her day, has been tamed.

*   *   *   *   *

Above Glen Canyon Dam ~ Lake Powell and its Canyons

By Tiffany Mapel

*"So we have a curious ensemble of wonderful features—
carved walls, royal arches, glens, alcove gulches, mounds,
and monuments. From which of these features shall we
select a name? We decide to call it Glen Canyon."*

~ John Wesley Powell, 1869

Glen Canyon Dam sits 15 miles upstream from Lees Ferry, which is mile zero on the river. All buoys on Lake Powell are numbered in miles in the distance they are from Glen Canyon Dam. Lake Powell extends approximately 186 miles upstream from Glen Canyon Dam when full, and has 96 major side canyons. Lake Powell is the second largest man-made reservoir in the U.S. Lake Mead, on the Colorado River downstream from Lake Powell, is the largest reservoir in the U.S.

Before Lake Powell, the Colorado River through Glen Canyon was used by several groups of people from the past. The first known inhabitants were the "Basketmaker" culture, followed by the "Anasazi," or Ancestral Puebloans. "Anasazi" is a Navajo word that means "Ancient Enemies." The word was applied to the Ancestral

Puebloan culture, and much to the chagrin of the Navajos, the word stuck. The Puebloan culture built small dwellings under alcoves, and high upon canyon walls for protection. Their ruins are evident in several canyons on Lake Powell. They thrived in canyon country for hundreds of years, but suddenly left the area around 1250 AD. No one is certain of their reasons for departure, but it is surmised that drought may have driven them out.

Other people who later called Glen Canyon home were the Navajo, Ute, and Piute Indians. As America was a young country and westward expansion brought settlers out west, people of European descent began to move in: fur trappers, gold seekers, cattlemen, and later, river runners. While this alone could be a topic for a whole new book, we won't go into great detail here.

Lake Powell was named for John Wesley Powell, (1834-1902) a one-armed Civil War veteran, and an explorer with a keen interest in science and geology. On an 1859 map of the United States published by Congress, the area of the Colorado River corridor was marked "unexplored." That alone piqued Powell's interest, and he soon organized his first trip, which set out on May 24, 1869 from Green River, Wyoming. With four boats and nine men, Powell and his crew set out to explore and map the region. Powell selected mountain men for this journey—men who were experienced in living off the land. Participants on Powell's first trip in 1869 included:

John Wesley Powell, Civil War Veteran, geologist, explorer
Walter H. Powell, J. W. Powell's brother, also a Civil War Captain
Oramel G. Howland, a printer, editor, and hunter
Seneca Howland, Oramel's younger brother
William H. Dunn, hunter/trapper from Colorado
John C. Sumner, Civil War soldier, hunter
George Y. Bradley, Civil War Lieutenant
Frank Goodman, stranger, Englishman—looking for adventure
William R. Hawkins, expedition cook, Civil War soldier
Andrew Hall, 19, Scottish, hunter/trapper

The 1869 trip on the Colorado River was treacherous, and Powell and his men nearly starved; much of their food supply was lost to rapids, or soaked in river water. Their boats constantly needed repairs. It seemed to be one struggle after another. One month into the trip, on July 5th, Frank Goodman informed Powell that he was leaving the journey—he'd had enough. Later, going through the unforgiving Grand Canyon, three more of Powell's men decided to climb out, rather than face more dangerous rapids. On August 28, 1869, brothers Oramel and Seneca Howland, and William Dunn, climbed out at what is today called "Separation Rapid" in the Grand Canyon. Some time after they had reached the rim, Shivwits Indians killed all three. Had they stayed with the expedition, only two days later they would have reached the Virgin River in Arizona, out of the Grand Canyon—and ultimately survived.

Almost immediately after the 1869 journey, Powell began to plan for his second journey. This time, better boats were used, and Powell selected professionals to accompany him. Congress funded the second journey, which was better organized for collecting information. The roster for the second expedition included:

John Wesley Powell, trip leader and lead geologist
Professor Almon H. Thompson, Powell's brother-in-law
E. O. Beaman, a photographer
J. F. Steward, assistant geologist
John "Jack" K. Hillers, photographer and boatman
Frederick S. Dellenbaugh, an artist and mapmaker
Stephen Vandiver Jones
F. M. Bishop
Frank Richardson, assistant geologist
Andrew Hattan
Clement Powell, assistant photographer

The explorers left Green River, Wyoming on May 22, 1871, and reached the Grand Canyon on September 30th. Jacob Hamblin, a Mormon with whom Powell was acquainted, cached supplies for the Powell expedition at Crossing of the Fathers in Glen Canyon.

The second expedition ended at the Paria River confluence for 1871. The crew spent the rest of the year and the first portion of 1872 mapping southern Utah and the Arizona Strip, the section of land northwest of the Grand Canyon. The trip resumed in August of 1872. The second expedition brought back considerably more information than the first. Surveys were taken for science and topography, sketches were drawn, photographs taken with cumbersome equipment, and detailed accounts of everything they observed were recorded. Places were officially named.

*   *   *   *   *

In order to become more familiar with Lake Powell, its history will give you perspective. Each major canyon will be discussed, with its mileage location, and pertinent history, if it is known. Some of these canyons still retain their mysteries to this day. Find your favorite canyon, and learn about its past. The numbers contained in parentheses () show how many miles each canyon is from Glen Canyon Dam, and are not necessarily the number of the buoy that marks each canyon.

Antelope Island (9) When the water of Lake Powell fills the **Castle Rock Cut** at 3580 and the Cut is navigable at 3584, it creates Antelope Island by connecting Wahweap Bay and Warm Creek Bay. Back in the early 1970s when the rising water joined those two basins, the island was called "San Carlos Island." In 1976 it was officially named "Antelope Island." The Castle Rock Cut was originally excavated down to 3622 back in the 1970s. Then again to 3615 in 1992 to remove sediment. Early in 2008 an Environmental Assessment was done to plan for further excavations. After a Finding of No Significant Impact (FONSI) and overwhelming majority of votes in favor for the project, the contract was awarded to the Brown Brothers of Loa, Utah. They began excavating in early 2009. They blasted down to 3580, as was the original plan. However, they could only excavate as far as the receding water level allowed—to about 3610. Excavated material was spread out near Castle Rock to blend in with the environment. The last time the Cut was excavated was in 2014 when it was taken down to the 3580 level. As Lake Powell's water level has fluctuated significantly from 2000 to 2021, the Castle Rock Cut has been usable most years, but unavailable when the water level drops below 3584. When usable, the Cut is about 120 feet wide, and about a mile long.

Antelope Canyon (4) This is the first canyon as you head east and upstream from Glen Canyon Dam. It has approximately 5 miles of waterway, and the best scenery is from the section that is on land. Tours through Antelope Canyon on land are by paid permit through the Navajo Nation, and with Navajo guides. One or two Navajo outfitters take tourists down into the "corkscrew" for surreal canyon beauty. Antelope Canyon is named for the wild Pronghorn antelope, which used to roam the area long ago. Antelope Canyon on land has two sections: upper and lower. The Navajo call the upper section "Tse' bighanilini," which means, "the place where water runs through rock." The Navajo name for the lower section is "Hasdestwazi," which means, "spiral rock arches."

Antelope Point Marina (5) This is Lake Powell's newest marina. It is owned and operated entirely by the Navajo Nation. It boasts the world's largest floating restaurant. The first phase of the marina complex opened in summer, 2004. The restaurant opened a year later.

Navajo Canyon (9) Powell's second expedition in 1871 stopped by this canyon, and Frederick Dellenbaugh named the small creek "Navajo Creek." This is the longest canyon on Lake Powell—30 miles. It branches into two other canyons: Navajo Creek to the east, and Chaol Canyon to the south. With many ruins in the canyon before Lake Powell, this was a popular canyon with the Indians.

Wahweap Bay (8) "Wahweap" is a Piute word that supposedly means "bitter water." Wahweap Bay was named for Wahweap Creek, which flowed toward the Colorado River before Lake Powell. At the mouth of Wahweap Canyon stood a 250-foot high sandstone pinnacle. Wahweap Creek flowed on one side, and the Colorado River on the other. The rock was named "Sentinel Rock" by John Wesley Powell's second Colorado River trip on October 18, 1871. At the base of Sentinel Rock, many river runners would inscribe their names and years. Bert Loper signed on the Wahweap Creek side of the rock, leaving testament to 41 years of his river passages. Other canyons branch off from Wahweap Bay: Wiregrass Canyon, Blue Pool Wash, Lone Rock Canyon, and Ice Cream Canyon.

Warm Creek Bay (16) Before Lake Powell, there was a small town called "Warm Springs" in the bottom of what is today Warm Creek Bay. Warm Creek Bay is named for the former town. As the water of Lake Powell rose, the remnants of the town's adobe walls were lost to the waves. Off Warm Creek Bay, Crosby Canyon is a branch off the northwest side. The Spencer Coal Mines were located in that area, and Charles Spencer used to fuel his gold dredge at Lees Ferry with coal mined at the Spencer Mines.

Gunsight Canyon (20) Gunsight Pass is a small passageway connecting Gunsight Canyon and Padre Canyon. An 1869 Mormon Militia group first called it "Gunsight Pass." The Militia group was in the area in pursuit of some Navajos, attempting to avenge a Navajo raid, which occurred in February of 1869. The Navajos were tracked to the Crossing of the Fathers sometime between February 25th and March 12th, but the Navajos escaped across the river. What is known as Gunsight Butte today was originally called "Steamboat Rock" by the Militia group. Later on, the name "Gunsight" was transferred to the butte itself, likely by river runners. Gunsight Pass remains today, and fills with water when Lake Powell is at full pool.

Gunsight Butte. T. Mapel photo, 2007.

Padre Canyon (21) Padre Canyon is named in honor of the two Franciscan Friars, Francisco Atanasio Dominguez and Silvestre Velez de Escalante, who took their party of explorers through the red rock country in search of a trade route from Santa Fe, New Mexico to Monterey, California in November of 1776. Their famous **"Crossing of the Fathers"** was at a slow, shallow section of the Colorado River before Lake Powell. This crossing was also referred to as "Ute Ford," as the Natives had been using it for centuries. The Spaniards called it "El Vado de los Padres." Today, Padre Bay covers a wide area over their former crossing. The Fathers were the first known white men in Glen Canyon. Incidentally, the Fathers and their group were stuck in a small canyon during a storm in November of 1776, just two miles west of the Colorado River. They were still searching for a place to cross the river. In a particular canyon, (*not this canyon—the actual canyon will not be named, to protect the site from further, modern-graffiti damage) they left an inscription on the Navajo Sandstone wall that read in a beautiful Spanish script: "Paso por aqui, 1776." This translates as "passed by here, 1776." It is the only known surviving inscription from the Dominguez/Escalante party, and exists above the 3700-msl high-water line.

Kane Creek Canyon (22) When Hollywood came to Glen Canyon in 1964 to film "The Greatest Story Ever Told," Kane Creek Canyon was the location. It was supposed to be the River Jordan in Biblical times. If you see the movie, you can get a glimpse of what the area looked like as Lake Powell was slowly filling. Kane Creek Canyon is named for Kane Creek, which flows through it. *Kane* itself is a popular name in Utah, as in Kane County, of which Lake Powell is a part. Colonel Thomas L. Kane was a great friend of the Mormon people in the late 1800s, lending his name to many Utah features.

Kane Wash (23) Kane wash is located next to Kane Creek, and runoff from the slick rock drains to meet up with Kane Creek. Kane Wash contains "Cookie Jar Rock," which was named by Irene Greene Johnson, daughter of Art Greene.

Labyrinth Canyon (19) This is a narrow, twisting canyon with a great slot at the end, and was so named by river runner Norman Nevills. This canyon is in Arizona and Utah.

Face Canyon (24) Face Canyon exists in both Arizona and Utah as well. It is south of Padre Bay. It was named by river runners for the various "facial" features that could be seen in the sandstone walls at the mouth of the canyon.

Reflections in Face Canyon. T. Mapel photo, 2007.

Face Canyon ending in a water-filled slot. T. Mapel photo, 2007.

Last Chance Bay (27) This is a large bay with many small, unnamed side branches. Two of the ones that are named are on the eastern side, Twitchell Canyon, and Little Valley Canyon. It was called "Last Chance" because it was one of the last chances to get off the river before the rapids started downstream. In the days of cattle operations in the area, it was also the "last chance" for your cattle to get reliable, clean drinking water.

West Canyon (26) West Canyon is both in Arizona and Utah. It was first called Beaver Canyon by the Kelly W. Trimble USGS Expedition of 1921. Bert Loper, who was part of that Expedition, caught a beaver there. West Canyon has a branch called Howland Canyon. Howland Canyon was named after the two Howland brothers, Oramel and Seneca, who were on Powell's first Colorado River exploration in 1869. West Canyon has one of the best slot hikes on the lake.

Neanderthal Cove (29) Also called "Camel Rock Cove," as Camel Rock sits directly across from the cove. The Neanderthal name inspiration is unknown.

Gregory Butte (30) Although this is not a canyon, but a butte, it is worth noting here. It was first called "Church Rock" by river runners, but was later named on the official USGS map in honor of Herbert Gregory, who studied the Glen Canyon region prior to Lake Powell. Upstream in Fiftymile Canyon of the Escalante, Gregory Natural Bridge, the only natural bridge to be inundated by Lake Powell, was also named in Mr. Gregory's honor. But once the bridge went under water, the butte at the southern end of the lake was then re-named for Herbert Gregory.

Friendship Cove (32) According to Stan Jones, every year the Rotary Club of Page, Arizona would invite other Rotary members throughout Arizona to a cookout. They would take everyone out by boat on newly formed Lake Powell. They would camp out and call it a "friendship meeting." Stan suggested they name it "Friendship Cove," since it wasn't on the map yet. Stan Jones was known as "Mr. Lake Powell," as he was one of the earlier explorers of the lake and surrounding area in the early 1960s. He documented his ramblings in journals and books, and created the main map of the lake that is still in use today. Before Lake Powell, a trio of river runners had called Friendship Cove "Cattail Canyon." This particular trio of river runners went through Glen Canyon with the Mexican Hat Expeditions from 1954-62. They called themselves "*We Three*," and are responsible for naming many of Lake Powell's present-day canyons.

Rock Creek (33) The name of Rock Creek was in use for this canyon as early as 1897. It was named for the boulder-strewn streambed, which posed a hazard to river runners. Rock Creek consists of three major branches: Rock Creek Bay, Middle Rock Creek, and Dry Rock

Creek. With Rock Creek Bay being the main branch, Middle Rock Creek and Dry Rock Creek are smaller. Dry Rock Creek also has the added interest of having a balanced rock in the back of the canyon.

Dungeon Canyon (38) The trio of river runners named this canyon because it was such a narrow canyon, and not a lot of light came through to the bottom. It was dark and cool, like a dungeon.

Grotto Canyon (39) Another canyon named by the trio of river runners because it was a short canyon ending in a plunge pool. Before Lake Powell, the end of this canyon had walls of maidenhair ferns and flowers surrounding the plunge pool.

Wetherill Canyon (39.5) This canyon was named for John Wetherill on later USGS maps. River runners had always called it "Catfish Canyon." John Wetherill was a trading post owner, and was also the first white man to ride under Rainbow Bridge. He was a guide on the first expedition in 1909 to see Rainbow Bridge.

Cornerstone Canyon (40) This canyon was named by the trio of river runners for the downstream side of the canyon that looked like a big building—like it was cut with a giant square edge. The canyon had straight walls that came right down to the ground.

Dangling Rope Canyon (40) Dangling Rope Canyon is just upstream from Cornerstone Canyon. It was named by the trio of river runners who discovered a miner's rope hanging down a cliff face in the back of the canyon. No one tried to climb the rope, however, as it didn't look to be very safe. This canyon also hosts the successful mid-lake marina called "Dangling Rope."

Dangling Rope Marina (40) Dangling Rope Marina is one of the most lucrative marinas in the western United States. This is the only mid-lake marina to re-fuel at on Lake Powell. This marina came online in 1983, after Rainbow Bridge Marina was moved to Dangling Rope Canyon for more space. This isolated marina is only serviced by barge from Wahweap at the south end of Lake Powell. Everything comes in by barge—gas, food, ice, and store items; trash and recyclables are taken out on the barge as well. Employees are housed in a facility just over the ridge from the marina. There are also NPS offices at the marina. At first, diesel generators powered Dangling Rope Marina. In 1996, Dangling Rope converted to solar. Now, the entire marina is powered by solar power; it is completely self-sufficient for electrical power.

Mountain Sheep Canyon (42) Charles Bernheimer named this canyon "Mountain Sheep Canyon" in 1924, as he looked down into the canyon from Cummings Mesa. He named it for all the desert bighorn sheep tracks he saw near the rim. Later on, river runners had called it both "False Entrance Canyon" and "Pick Ax Canyon." It was officially called Mountain Sheep after Lake Powell was formed.

Balanced Rock Canyon (43) This canyon was named by the trio of river runners for the small, balanced rocks they found there, where the ground around them had eroded away, and they were left on small pinnacles.

Little Arch Canyon (43) This canyon was also named by the trio of river runners for a small arch they found at the rim of the canyon. Before it became known as Little Arch, the trio called this canyon "Fern Glen," for all the maidenhair ferns that bedecked the walls. The arch on the rim is unofficially called "Carrot Top Arch," named by Stan Jones in honor of his wife, a redhead named Alice.

Driftwood Canyon (46) Driftwood Canyon was so called because of the driftwood mat that clogged the entrance to the canyon before Lake Powell. The trio of river runners also named it.

Cathedral Canyon (46) The trio of river runners named this canyon, too. Cathedral Butte stands near the mouth of the canyon. At the end of this canyon was a large chamber with an "altar" rock, which reminded them of a great cathedral.

Cascade Canyon (47) Before Lake Powell, this canyon was known as "Kluckhohn Canyon" for Clyde Kluckhohn, who led a Glen Canyon Expedition in 1928. The trio of river runners called it "68 Mile

Canyon," but Tad Nichols, who was part of the *"We Three"* group, named it Cascade Canyon because it had many shelves and cascades all the way down the canyon.

Forbidding Canyon (49) This canyon became known as "Forbidding" after a failed attempt to use it as a route to Rainbow Bridge. Rainbow Bridge exists up Bridge Canyon, a branch of Forbidding. Bridge Creek drains under Rainbow Bridge, and joins up with Aztec Creek, which flows down Forbidding Canyon.

Rainbow Bridge National Monument (51) Rainbow Bridge was called *"Nonnezoshe"* by the Navajo, which described it as a "rainbow turned to stone." The local Indian tribes had previously known about it, but no white men had seen it until 1909; previous to that date, no recorded sightings from white men existed. It's possible that miners knew about it before 1909. In that year, two parties set out to see the rock Rainbow somewhere near the foot of Navajo Mountain: one group under government surveyor W.B. Douglass, and another group with a University of Utah Dean, Byron Cummings. The two parties ran into each other, and joined forces. Along with a guide named John Wetherill, two Indians also came along as guides: a Ute named Jim Mike, and a Piute named Nasja Begay. Rainbow Bridge was sighted and officially recorded by white men for the first time on August 14, 1909. President Taft designated Rainbow Bridge as a National Monument in 1910.

In 1909, William B. Douglass measured the height of Rainbow Bridge at 309 feet, and the length of the span at 278 feet. These measurements remained in place for many years. Later, with more sophisticated measuring equipment, the true height of the Bridge was revealed: it is 291 feet high, and the span is 275 feet. The Bridge also rises or falls by as much as 0.38 inches from summer to winter. This is due to moisture and temperature, as the sandstone expands and contracts.

At the southwest base of Navajo Mountain, there used to exist a building known as Rainbow Lodge. It was a welcome stop for land-based tourists sometime around the 1940s or 1950s, and was 14 miles away by trail to Rainbow Bridge. Senator Barry Goldwater owned the primary interest in Rainbow Lodge at the time. As Lake Powell was coming closer to fruition, Mr. Goldwater realized that the land-based tourism was going to decline sharply. And it did. Water access was so much easier for tourists.

Tourism at Lake Powell really began to ramp up in the mid 1970s. Art Greene's *Canyon Tours* to Rainbow Bridge ran all day, and later Art offered half-day tours to accommodate growing numbers of tourists starting in the late 1960s. In the 1970s, Art was the only officially licensed tour operator on Lake Powell. By 1976, visitation to Lake Powell topped more than 65,000 people.

The Navajo Nation borders the 160 acres of Rainbow Bridge National Monument on three sides. Consequently, the Nation wanted its share of concessions for the new Monument, and they also wanted to be in on any decisions affecting the Monument. From the 1950s to the 1990s, the National Park Service and the Navajo Nation tried to see eye to eye on how to run the Monument. *The Rainbow Bridge Mission 66 Prospectus* was submitted on April 23, 1956, before Lake Powell had even begun to fill. It called for enlarging the Monument's boundaries for necessary facilities; trail improvements, and utility and residential buildings for permanent and seasonal staff. A visitor center was planned, including a campfire ring, campground, and signage. Today, when you visit Rainbow Bridge, these things are not there—and never were. Today you get a dock to pull up to, floating restrooms, an information kiosk, and perhaps a ranger to answer interpretive questions, and keep visitors on the trail.

As Lake Powell begun to fill, there was very little Monument supervision that first decade. The Superintendent of Navajo National Monument was doing double-duty looking after both his own and Rainbow Bridge National Monument. Finally, management was transferred to Glen Canyon National Recreation Area in 1964. The management would be divided between Reclamation and the National Park Service. On August 5, 1964, it was determined that the Superintendent of Glen Canyon would manage Rainbow Bridge National Monument. However, Glen Canyon National Recreation Area was later officially established in 1972, and very little legislative work in the NRA was done prior to this date.

Rainbow Bridge. T. Mapel photo, 1998.

Rainbow Bridge Marina There also used to be a marina, known as Rainbow Bridge Marina, just inside Forbidding Canyon as Lake Powell was rising in 1964. It lasted in that location until about 1983, when it was towed to the present-day location of Dangling Rope Canyon. Being in the narrow Forbidding Canyon with all that boat traffic made for tight quarters with boats trying to fill up, and boats trying to get beyond the marina into the canyon. Art Greene had the concessions on Lake Powell covered; he opened Wahweap Marina, built the new Rainbow Bridge Marina there, and had it towed uplake to Forbidding Canyon. Woody Reiff was the first manager of Rainbow Bridge Marina, working for Art Greene. Back in 1966, fuel on the dock there was about 49 cents per gallon. Sometimes, if no one was there to take your money, gas purchases were on the honor system. You took what gas you needed, and you put your money in the box on the dock. It worked that way for many years. Obviously, that system would not work today.

Rainbow Marina. Bureau of Reclamation photo.

Twilight Canyon (50.5) Twilight was known to various river runners as "Boulder Canyon," likely due to the large granite cobbles that lay in its streambed that previously tumbled down from the Kaiparowits Plateau above. However, river man Norman Nevills came up with the name "Twilight," and that name made it on the official USGS map.

Secret Canyon (50) On the official USGS map, Secret Canyon is called "Oak Canyon." However, on Stan Jones's map, it is called "Secret," since he named it. "Secret" seems to be a more fitting name, as the entrance to the narrow canyon isn't that obvious. It is a narrow waterway, too narrow for a houseboat. Secret Canyon is a south branch from Oak Bay. The Navajo had called this canyon "Blackwater," due to the black-colored algae in the streambed, but the *We Three* river runners called it "Wishbone Canyon," due to the way the mouth of the canyon diverted its steam *upstream* next to the Colorado River before draining into the larger river a bit further on.

Oak Bay/Oak Canyon (51) What is called "Secret Canyon" on the USGS map is called "Oak Canyon" on Stan Jones's map. This is a short canyon off the back of Oak Bay. It was likely called "Oak" because of the many scrub oak trees in the back of the canyon.

Anasazi Canyon (52.5) In the 1920s, Norman Nevills had named this canyon "Mystery Canyon," for the set of Moqui steps that go up one wall and seem to go nowhere. Hence, the mystery. However, the name "Anasazi" became the official name. There are two branches off Anasazi: Lehi and Moepitz Canyons. Frank E. Masland Jr. suggested the name in 1959 after a Piute named Dan Lehi led an expedition in the area. Masland also suggested "Moepitz," as it is Piute for "owl." At lower water, somewhere in the 3585-range, a double set of natural bridges in the Navajo Sandstone span Lehi Canyon that you can boat underneath.

Lehi Canyon double bridges. T. Mapel photo, 2006.

Boating under a Lehi Bridge. T. Mapel photo, 2005.

Morning reflections in Anasazi Canyon. T. Mapel photo, 2009.

Hidden Passage Canyon (55) River runners had named this canyon due to the hidden entrance from the Colorado River. It was a narrow canyon with thick foliage and sandstone fins at its entrance. If you didn't know the entrance was there, you could easily miss it.

Music Temple Canyon (55) Directly across the channel from Hidden Passage, lays Music Temple. John Wesley Powell himself named this canyon, on his first Colorado River voyage in 1869. As they pulled in to set camp, he and his men noticed that it was a lovely amphitheater in the sandstone that could seat thousands. Powell's brother, Walter, noticed the amazing acoustics of the canyon that evening around the campfire, and Powell named it "Music Temple."

Reflection Canyon (56) This canyon was previously known as "Cottonwood Gulch." In fact, on some maps, it still lists the right branch as such. Both branches of the canyon held ruins before Lake Powell. It could likely have gotten its *Reflection* name from being directly across the channel from the San Juan—a reflection of the large river.

San Juan River Arm (57) The San Juan River was first called by that name by a Spanish explorer known as Don Juan Maria de Rivera in 1765. It was also called the Navajo River, and Rio San Juan. The San Juan River is a major tributary to the Colorado River. Its headwaters begin in the San Juan Mountains on the Continental Divide on Wolf Creek Pass near Pagosa Springs, Colorado. In Navajo mythology, the San Juan is known as *"Old Age River," "One-With-a-Long-Body,"* or *"One-With-a-Wide-Body."* Even before the San Juan became the northern boundary of the Navajo Reservation in 1884, the Navajo saw it as a safe line of separation from the northern Utes and the white men. At full pool, the navigable portion of the San Juan River extends 56 miles up stream from its confluence with the Colorado.

> **Nasja Canyon** (5.5 miles—from the confluence) This canyon was named for Nasja Begay, a Piute who was on the Rainbow Bridge expedition in 1909.

> **Bald Rock Canyon** This canyon is a tributary to Nasja Canyon. This canyon also contains the original trail to Rainbow Bridge.

> **Cha Canyon** (11) In the Navajo language, "Cha" means "beaver." So there must have been beaver present to inspire the naming of this canyon.

> **Trail Canyon** (13) This canyon offered good access to the San Juan, so there were several trails built in it down to the

river. This was during the mining days. In 1908 prospectors came down in search of oil and uranium. Later, a major landslide split the main trail in half.

Wilson Creek Canyon (13.5) This canyon was named for the Wilson family, who were prominent settlers and stockmen in the area back in the 1800s. Wilson Mesa northeast of the canyon is also named for them.

Desha Canyon (14.5) "Desha" is a Navajo word for "curved." Herbert E. Gregory suggested this canyon name in 1915.

Deep Canyon (16) This canyon was named for its obvious feature—it is a deep and narrow canyon.

Piute Canyon (19) This was named in honor of the Piute Indians who live in the area.

Neskahi Wash (22) In Navajo, "Neskahi" means "fat." Apparently, this canyon is where the Navajos used to fatten up their sheep in preparation for ceremonies.

Wild burros in Neskahi Wash of the San Juan. T. Mapel photo, 2009.

Great Bend (26) This is a long gooseneck of the river that takes nine miles to get around.

Alcove Canyon (30.5) This canyon was named by Hugh D. Miser of the Kelly W. Trimble USGS Expedition of 1921, for all the alcoves contained within the canyon walls.

Spencer Camp (36) This was named for Charles Spencer, who set up a rock-crushing operation for mining in 1908.

Zahn Bay (39) This was named for the Zahn brothers, Otto and Hector. They were miners in the early 1900s.

Nokai Canyon (42) "Nokai" is a Navajo word meaning "Mexican Waters."

Castle Creek Canyon (44) This canyon was used by Native American tribes to access the San Juan River. Castle Creek flows through the canyon, and was given its name from some nearby castle-like Indian ruins near Green Water Spring. The Hole-in-the-Rock expedition passed through this canyon in February 1880 on their way to settle Bluff, Utah.

Copper Canyon (44.5) This canyon was named for the extensive copper mining that occurred there. Gold and silver were also mined here in the late 1880s.

Mikes Canyon (48.5) This canyon was named for Jim Mike, a Ute who was on the 1909 Rainbow Bridge expedition as a guide.

Piute Farms Wash (52) At one time, this was a large Indian settlement near the San Juan River. After Lake Powell was formed, this open section of water used to contain the first Navajo-owned marina, San Juan Marina. Unfortunately, it washed away in a flood in 1989. It was never rebuilt in that location. Nowadays, the new Antelope Point Marina toward the south end of Lake Powell is the new and improved Navajo-owned marina.

Clay Hills Crossing (56) This is the end of navigable water when Lake Powell is near full pool. This is a good take-out point for river rafters, who put in at either Bluff or Mexican Hat. A dirt road goes from Clay Hills Crossing about 13 miles back up to Highway 276 at Clay Hills Pass. When full, Lake Powell covers Clay Hills Crossing to a depth of about 75 feet. The lake extends 13 miles upriver, nearly to the mouth of Grand Gulch.

Llewellyn Gulch (63) This canyon was named for Llewellyn Harris, a Utah Mormon pioneer. Mr. Harris also left his inscription within the canyon, "L. Harris, March 29, 1888," although it is very faint and difficult to see.

Cottonwood Canyon (65) This canyon was named by the Hole in the Rock party, as it was where they exited the Colorado River corridor, and headed for their destination of settling Bluff, Utah, along the San Juan River. In some places, you can still see the old Mormon wagon road. There are interpretive signs along the trail, placed there by NPS.

Hole In The Rock (65) This cleft in the canyon rim saw a lot of excitement back in 1879. There were about 230 to 250 Mormon settlers—men, women, and children, in 83 wagons, with about 1,000 head of cattle and horses making this trip. It was called the San Juan Mission Party. When they arrived at the precipice overlooking the Colorado River, the crack that was to become *Hole in the Rock* was their only option down to the river crossing. Using gunpowder, the men began blasting the crack wider, preparing it for the wagons. It took 60 days to prepare the dugway at Hole in the Rock before the wagons were lowered down. The slope down to the river was anywhere from 25 to 45 degrees, and amazingly, all wagons, people, and animals made the trip down to the river.

Back then, there was a ferry near Hole in the Rock run by none other than Charles Hall and his sons. He built the ferry himself using trees near the river, and the ferry platform was large enough for two of the wagons at a time. Hall would later run another ferry at Hall's Crossing, 35 miles upstream from Hole in the Rock, and is the namesake of the current-day marina. Visitors to Hole in the Rock today should note that time has taken its toll on the old wagon route. It looks very different than it did in 1879-1880. Erosion has changed it, and many large boulders have fallen down from the rim. You can still hike it today on foot, though. When you see steps carved into the sandstone, miners of the Hoskininni Mining Company later picked those in. The miners were searching for gold in the bars along the Colorado River, and used the Hole in the Rock route up until 1900.

With 83 wagons, nearly 250 people, and 1000 animals, it took quite a while to get everyone ferried across the river safely. Once on the other shore at Cottonwood Canyon, the Mormon pioneers had to build more road base and move large boulders so the wagons could roll as smooth as possible up through Register Rocks. When the water level of Lake Powell dropped to its lowest point in the early spring of 2005, you could still see some of this old road base. Rocks are still stacked neatly, and you can see remnants of the old road the wagons took to get up through Cottonwood Canyon. As the pioneers paused at Register Rocks, some of the party took time to inscribe their names in the nearby rock. The wagon train then headed up Cottonwood Canyon, toward their destination of Bluff, Utah. On their way, they wintered near Lake Pagahrit (also called Hermit Lake) at the head of Lake Canyon. The San Juan Mission party journey was to take six weeks, and it ended up taking six months. The travelers were thoroughly exhausted by then. Amazingly, no lives were lost on this journey and three babies were born during those six months.

Ribbon Canyon (67) This canyon was originally called "Echo Canyon" by miners in the 1880s. The trio of river runners of the *"We Three"* group called it "Ribbon Canyon" for the lovely purple-colored water stain that extended quite a length down the slickrock bottom of the canyon.

Escalante River Arm (69) The Escalante River flows through the southern Utah town of Escalante—both named for Father Silvestre

Velez de Escalante, a 1776 explorer. At the mouth of the Escalante River confluence with the Colorado, high upon the shore was a large, flat rock, which contained a map of the Escalante etched into the sandstone. River runners likely put it there to inform other river runners what was upstream. Incidentally, the Escalante River was the last western river "discovered" and mapped, by Powell's second expedition. Almon Thompson, Powell's brother-in-law, gave the Escalante its name on June 4th, 1872, although Father Escalante and his expedition were never in this area. Before it was called Escalante, Thompson had given the small river a name that thankfully did not stay: Potato Creek, or Potato Valley Creek—a tribute to the wild potatoes found growing at the head of the canyon.

Indian Creek Canyon (1.5) The first canyon in the Escalante Arm is about a mile up on the left. It is a short canyon that ends in a large wall with no slots to climb out of. Edson Alvey noted that Indian remains were found in this canyon. It was also reportedly used as a place for barter between the early white settlers and the Indians.

Clear Creek Canyon (2.5) This canyon was named for the year-round running stream that has cut an interesting path forming many waterfalls and waterpockets on its way down the canyon. **Cathedral in the Desert** is one of the most popular sites on Lake Powell, and is contained in Clear Creek Canyon. Cathedral in the Desert was named by Bob Fullmer, a photographer from Los Angeles (year unknown).

Cathedral in the Desert, Clear Creek Canyon, Escalante drainage,
April 2005. The water was at its lowest point that year. T. Mapel photo.

Cathedral in the Desert, two months later, spring runoff raised
the water level significantly. T. Mapel photo, June 2005.

Davis Gulch (5.5) This canyon was named for John Davis, a
cattleman from Escalante, Utah. Two miles up this canyon is
LaGorce Arch, named for Dr. John Oliver LaGorce, a former
president of the National Geographic Society. The arch was

first called "Moqui Window" before it became known as LaGorce Arch. Roosevelt Arch was another name that was used. Davis Gulch is also known for being the last spot where young artist/adventurer Everett Ruess lived, before he disappeared in November 1934.

*The mystery of the disappearance of Everett Ruess in 1934 made news once again in May 2009. The story broke in the April/May 2009 issue of National Geographic Adventure. Back in 2008, a Navajo grandfather told a story to his adult granddaughter of witnessing a young white man's murder by a trio of Utes back in 1934. The granddaughter's younger brother became interested in his grandfather's story. The elder Navajo, Aneth Nez, claimed to have buried the young white man in haste and refrained from telling his family, until recently. In the Navajo culture, you are not supposed to touch or go near dead bodies. Nez's grandson was intrigued and looked for the burial site, which was in Comb Ridge, southeast Utah. He found it within a crevice but did not touch the bones. He alerted the FBI and other authorities. Specialists ruled out a Navajo burial, since the skull wasn't facing east. Forensic anthropologists soon carefully excavated the site. After contacting the living relatives of Everett Ruess, University of Colorado anthropologists obtained DNA samples for testing. One test confirmed that the remains were indeed Ruess. Another skeptical scientist felt that another test was necessary. Additional DNA testing ruled that the skeleton was not Ruess. And so, there is still no closure to the 75-year mystery. While Everett was alive, perhaps he unintentionally prophesied his own death by writing, "When I go, I leave no trace." Wherever he ended up, may Everett rest in peace.

LaGorce Arch in Davis Gulch, Escalante drainage.
T. Mapel photo, 2005.

Fiftymile Canyon (7) This canyon was named as such because it is located 50 miles from Escalante, Utah. This canyon contains **Gregory Natural Bridge**, the only natural bridge to be inundated by Lake Powell water, and was named for Herbert E. Gregory (1869-1952). On a river trip in 1940 in which Norman Nevills and Barry Goldwater were present, both of these men are given credit for naming Gregory Natural Bridge. Fiftymile Canyon also used to be known as "Soda Gulch." This canyon has a year-round running stream in it, originating from Fiftymile Spring at the base of the Straight Cliffs of the Kaiparowits Plateau.

Willow Creek Canyon (9.5) This canyon was named for the abundance of willows that line the year-round running stream. This canyon contains **Broken Bow Arch**, discovered and named by Edson Alvey, for the Native hunting weapon found there. Willow Creek also has two tributaries: Bishop Canyon, and Fortymile Gulch. The latter was named by the Hole in the Rock pioneers for the mileage it was from where the Gulch crosses the Hole in the Rock Road to Escalante.

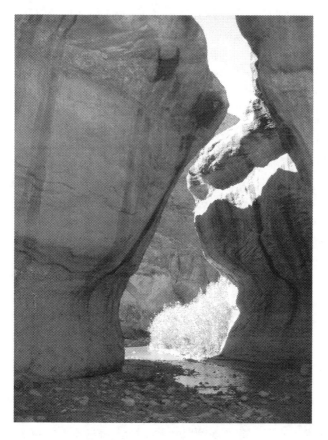

Willow Creek Canyon, Escalante drainage.
Hiking above the high-water line. T. Mapel photo, October 2007.

Explorer Canyon (12) This canyon contains everything: petroglyphs, arches, and even fossilized dinosaur footprints. Edson Alvey discovered and named **Zane Grey Arch**, although Zane Grey himself had never been in this particular canyon. This canyon was so named for a group of scouts from Salt Lake City who explored the area.

Garces Island (12) Also known as "Garces Rock." This is a large sandstone monolith, and water goes all the way around it when the lake is fairly full. It is also a popular camping spot, usually surrounded by nice sandy beaches. When the water level is sufficient, water skiers can do laps around the rock. It is likely that Garces Island is named for Francisco Garces, a Spanish Franciscan missionary, who attempted to settle a colony on the Colorado River among the Quechan, or Yuma Indians. The warlike Indians clashed with the Spanish settlers, and in July of 1781, Garces and his men were killed.

Fence and Cow Canyons (15) These two canyons share a mouth; Fence is to the right, and Cow is to the left. They were likely given these names back in the late 1800s to early 1900s. Cow Canyon was named for all the "wild" cows, which roamed the canyon. Fence Canyon was named because at one time, the whole canyon was fenced as a pasture.

Coyote Gulch (21) This canyon was named for one of the natural features in it. Coyote Gulch contains two impressive arches: **Jacob Hamblin Arch**, and **Coyote Natural Bridge**. The first arch was named for a Mormon explorer back in 1871, who helped the Powell survey. The second one was given the coyote name, since coyotes were frequently spotted in the area. Before it was known as Coyote, Escalante stockmen called it Lobo Arch—a tribute to a lone grey wolf that roamed the canyon at that time.

Stevens Canyon (23.5) This canyon contains another large arch, **Stevens Arch**, which is sometimes called Skyline Arch. When Lake Powell is at full pool, you can boat within sight of this magnificent arch. This canyon was named for Al Stevens, who used to run cattle in this canyon.

Bowns/Long Canyons (74.5) These two canyons share a mouth. As you boat in, Bowns is the left fork, and Long is the right fork. From Bowns Canyon, the Bennetts Oil Field Trail climbs up out of the canyon. Bowns is named for William Bown. Long Canyon is named for Horace J. Long, a mining engineer from Bingham, Utah.

View toward the Rincon from the Kayenta ledges in Bowns Canyon.
T. Mapel photo, October 2005.

Rincon (77) The Rincon is an old Colorado River channel that wrapped around a large butte. "Rincon" is Spanish for "corner." This section of the river was an oxbow, and the river ate through the narrow section millions of years ago. It is also surmised that perhaps an earthquake long ago may have helped to collapse a good portion of the Waterpocket Fold, which also helped to alter the river's course into a straighter line. Since the old Rincon river channel hasn't been used for a few million years, it has filled in with sand dunes, and later, cattle and jeep trails. The Rincon area is a popular camping area, and has good fishing.

Looking downlake from the Rincon. T. Mapel photo, March 2008.

Looking uplake from the Rincon. T. Mapel photo, March 2008.

Flying Eagle Cove (78) This is a new name for the small cove just to the northeast of the Rincon. There is a large natural bridge called "**Aleson Arch**" up near the rim that is located on the northeast side of the Rincon, and just south of the mouth of Iceberg Canyon. It was named for river runner Harry Aleson (1918-1972). Aleson, however, had a different name in mind for the arch: "Flying Eagle Bridge" or "Hanging Valley Bridge." The cove was named for his bridge name idea.

Iceberg Canyon (78) The *"We Three"* trio of river runners named this canyon "Iceberg" due to the cold, deep pools at its mouth before Lake Powell. If you wanted to get further into the canyon to explore it, you must first pass through the cold pools. It was not for the faint of heart. Before it became officially Iceberg, this canyon was called Wilson Canyon, as it cut into Wilson Mesa.

Slick Rock Canyon (81) This canyon was named for the many vertical sentinel rocks along the high Navajo Sandstone walls. It also contains a few ruins: one restored, and one that is fenced off.

Annies Canyon (83.5) Barry Goldwater named this canyon while he was on a Colorado River trip through Glen Canyon in 1940. He called it "Ann's Canyon," as a tribute to a fellow river runner, Ann Rosner.

Lake Canyon (89) This canyon was called "Lake Canyon" due to the natural lakes at the head of the canyon, particularly Lake Pagahrit, which overflowed its banks and flooded on November 1st of 1915, after days of heavy rains. In Piute, "Pagahrit" means "standing water." Lake Pagahrit was also called Hermit Lake. Lake Canyon contained many Native American dwellings and artifacts before Lake Powell. The most notable ruin was called "Wasp House," and was a square ruin tucked into an alcove.

Lost Eden Canyon (92.5) This beautiful canyon is just downstream from the mouth of Halls Creek Bay. Its left branch ends in a huge alcove, which has a nice, high waterfall after rainstorms. River runner Harry Aleson married Dorothy Donaldson Keyes in an alcove in this canyon. Ken Sleight and Otis "Dock" Marston were present for the nuptials. Ken suggested "Little Eden" as a name for the canyon, because of its immense beauty.

Storm-borne waterfall in Lost Eden Canyon.
T. Mapel photo, September 2007.

Halls Creek Bay (93) Charles T. Hall lends his name to Halls Creek Bay, and also to present-day **Halls Crossing Marina**. Prior to the name Halls Creek, it was known as Hoxie Creek, named for Richard L. Hoxie of the Lieutenant George M Wheeler Survey of 1872-73. It was still known as Hoxie Creek as late as 1924. Before Lake Powell, the old site of Halls Ranch was up near the head of the canyon, before it turned into narrows. Charles Halls had a small farm there in 1881. About a mile or two down the canyon from the Halls Ranch was the old Baker Ranch site, also known as the Smith Ranch. At full pool, the Baker Ranch is covered with water, but the Halls Ranch site was never covered by Lake Powell. Charles Hall formerly ran the ferry at Hole in the Rock, much further downstream. After the San Juan Mission Party crossing in 1879-80, Hall moved his ferry service upstream to a more accessible location, Halls Crossing. The Halls ferry was in service from 1881-1884.

Charles Hall Ferry (94) The only ferry on Lake Powell is the *Charles Hall*. It goes between Halls Crossing and Bullfrog daily, departing each marina every other hour during peak season, mid-May through mid-September. The ferry route is 3.1 miles, and takes approximately 30 minutes. It can carry up to 150 people and 22 vehicles. The *Charles Hall* was put into service in April of 2001. There was also another ferry, the *John Atlantic Burr*, which served Lake Powell for 20 years. In 2006, the *John Atlantic Burr* was sold to British Columbia in Canada, and shipped up there in four pieces.

The John Atlantic Burr Ferry, spotted near the Rincon on its journey downlake to Page, AZ. It will be sectioned into four pieces, and shipped up to British Columbia, where it will be re-assembled and put back into service. T. Mapel photo, October 2, 2005.

Bullfrog Bay (94) The bay and the current-day **Bullfrog Marina** are named for Bullfrog Creek, which flowed into the Colorado. Bullfrog Creek's drainage begins on the south side of Mount Hillers in the Henry Range, north of Lake Powell. Bullfrog Creek was likely the moniker given by miners. An 1873 survey party originally called Bullfrog Creek "Pine Alcove Creek."

Stanton Canyon (94) This canyon is situated on the northeastern side of Bullfrog Bay. It was named for Robert Brewster Stanton, who initially wanted to survey the Grand Canyon for a possible railroad. The mining bug bit him, so his next project was to run a pricey gold dredge operation in the Colorado River. The dredge only worked for about six months, and then Stanton's *Hoskininni Mining Company* went broke. The dredge was then left rusting and in disrepair in the river at the mouth of Stanton Canyon. River runners would stop by as tourists to see this piece of history. It is now under the water of Lake Powell.

Moki Canyon (99) Also called "Moqui Canyon," so either spelling is correct. "Moqui" is a Hopi word, meaning "the people," and is pronounced "mo-qwi." Moki is also a Hopi word that means "dead." This canyon contained over one hundred sites of ruins before Lake Powell, so it was a popular place for the Ancient Ones. Prospectors likely named it, as they probably noticed the abundance of ruins in the canyon, and attributed them to the "Moki" culture as it was called at that time. As you boat into Moki, you'll come to fork after about a mile. The left branch is called North Gulch, and the right branch is still Moki. It goes for another mile or two and has a few cattle trail exits to the rim up the sand slides. Before Lake Powell, river runners referred to Moki Canyon as "Mysterious Canyon." Excavation and study of ruins were done in 1929 by Bernheimer, Wetherill, and Johnson.

Hansen Creek Canyon (104) This canyon was named for a pair of prospectors back in 1888, two brothers by the name of N. and Theodore Hansen. The canyon was also used as wagon access during the placer mining days of Glen Canyon, from about 1884 to 1900. Miners would then spread out to either Smith Bar or California Bar along the Colorado River.

Crystal Spring Canyon (105) This inlet is directly across from Hansen Creek Canyon. Two explorers called it "Beaver Canyon" in 1955 for all the felled trees and beaver ponds the canyon contained. Otis "Dock" Marston suggested the name "Crystal Spring Canyon," so as not to confuse it with "Cha Canyon" up in the San Juan. ("Cha" means "beaver" in Navajo).

Smith Fork Canyon (106.5) This canyon was likely named for the Smith brothers, who were prospectors in the late 1800s. Smith Bar was also likely named for them. Before Lake Powell, Smith Fork Canyon was an important route for native people as a connection from the Henry Mountains to other points in Glen Canyon, particularly Forgotten Canyon.

Forgotten Canyon (106.5) This canyon was labeled "Forgotten" as it was inadvertently left off the 1922 USGS map. Forgotten Canyon contains the restored "**Defiance House Ruins**," so called for the warrior pictographs high on the wall above the ruins. In 1959, river runners Harry Aleson and Dick Sprang "discovered" the Defiance House Ruins. Certainly, others had seen it before, but these two were the first to document it. Jesse Jennings, an archaeologist, is credited with naming Defiance House in 1959 on a survey of Glen Canyon.

Knowles Canyon (108) This canyon was named for either Henry or Emery Knowles, both cattlemen who ran herds on Mancos Mesa, east of Good Hope Bay around 1890.

Warm Springs Canyon (110) This canyon was named by early day prospectors, although no warm springs existed in the canyon. It did have a year-round running stream and a nice waterhole that was a popular spot for river runners to stop and fill their canteens.

Cedar Canyon (110) Charles L. Bernheimer noted in 1929 that this canyon "has no cedar." So apparently, the name stuck.

Sevenmile Canyon (113.5) This canyon was named for the distance it was in relation to Ticaboo Creek. There was an old cabin located across the river from the mouth of Sevenmile. It was called the "Ryan Cabin," and was built by either Mike Ryan or Timothy O'Keefe during the late 1800s gold rush.

Good Hope Bay (119) This large bay was named for Good Hope Bar, the gravel bar that was on the upstream end of this 3-mile wall. Back in the mining days from 1884-1900, miners would work their claims, all for a bit of "flour" gold. Good Hope Mesa is located on the southeast slopes of Mount Ellsworth.

Ticaboo Canyon (122) "Ticaboo" supposedly means "friendly" in either Navajo or Piute, and this canyon was named as such by Cass Hite. Hite was a prospector who arrived in Glen Canyon in September of 1883. He built his house about a mile up Ticaboo Creek. There are many branches to Ticaboo: the left branch is called *South Fork*; the middle branch of Ticaboo Creek splits into three other branches at its head—*Middle Fork, North Fork, and East Fork*; and finally, the right branch is called *Peshliki Fork*. Cass had befriended a Navajo Chief named Hoskininni. The Chief called Hite "Pish-La-ki," which meant, "silver man." Cass Hite started his own farm with the good, clear water from Ticaboo Creek, and ran a store and post office at Hite City, which was at the mouth of Trachyte Canyon, upstream. He lived in Ticaboo Canyon until his death in 1914 at age 69. He was buried near his house and his grave is below the water of Lake Powell. Currently, a floating gravestone commemorates Cass Hite at Ticaboo Canyon. Cass Hite lends his name to the Hite Marina, 16 miles upstream from Ticaboo.

Red Canyon/Blue Notch (126) Red Canyon sits on the eastern shore of Good Hope Bay, and was named for its stunning red rock country. It was an easy access point to the Colorado River, and had many trails. Back in the 1880s, it was a popular canyon for gold and copper mining. In the 1950s, uranium was discovered in the Chinle Formation. Castle Butte, a prominent feature of northern Lake Powell, sits at the mouth of Red Canyon, and the head of Good Hope Bay. Red Canyon was named for the red rock coloring. Blue Notch is the northern canyon off Good Hope Bay, and was the site of the old uranium mines. Blue Notch was named for the predominant soil in the area, a blue-colored clay. In Colorado River history, Bert Loper was a well-known river man in Glen Canyon who made his home at the mouth of Red Canyon. He affectionately called his small log house his "Hermitage."

Scorup Canyon (127) This canyon was named for two prominent cattlemen brothers in early Glen Canyon history, Al and Jim Scorup. The Scorups ran cattle in the Glen Canyon region for nearly a half a century, taking over cattle operations from the Bluff Pool, which was the major cattle operation at the time.

Fourmile Canyon (131) This canyon was named for the mileage it was from Hite City.

Two Mile Canyon (133) This canyon was named for the mileage it was from Hite City.

Trachyte Canyon (135) Almon Thompson on Powell's second expedition named this canyon and creek on June 20th, 1871, for the light colored volcanic rock in the area, known as "Trachyte." Trachyte Canyon offered easy access to the Colorado River, as miners frequently used this route. Cass Hite's "Dandy Crossing" was located at the mouth of Trachyte, as was the original Hite City. Later, Arthur Chaffin moved to Hite in 1932, and operated his ferry at the same place as the Dandy Crossing. This was a useful connection on the road from Hanksville to Blanding. Arthur Chaffin operated his ferry from September 17, 1946 to June 5, 1964. That was closing day for the ferry, as the water of newly formed Lake Powell was rising fast.

White/Farley Canyons (136) These two canyons share a mouth. On the south shore at White Canyon at approximately 3600 feet in elevation, sat an old ruin called "Fort Moqui." It was named in the gold rush days by miners. At full pool, this ruin is covered by 100 feet of water. Cass Hite is said to have named White Canyon when he arrived with Chief Hoskininni and his band of Navajos in 1883. Seeing the stark white bands of sandstone against the red backdrop, Cass proclaimed it "White Canyon." Back in the uranium mining days, a uranium mill and small town were built at the mouth of the canyon. People lived there from about 1948 to 1954. The town was actually called "White Canyon," and had a post office, store, and housing for all the uranium workers. Farley Canyon was named for Tom Farley who ran cattle in the region during the late 1800s. It was noted that outlaws typically used Farley Canyon as a river crossing, rather than use the ferry downstream at Dandy Crossing.

North Wash (139) John Wesley Powell called this canyon "Pass Canyon" in his diary of 1871. Stephen Vandiver Jones, also on Powell's 1871 expedition, called it "Lost Creek Gulch." In the early 1900s, it was called "Crescent Creek," coined by miners. It was later called "North Wash" since it drains the northern part of the Henry Mountains. It also offered easy access to the Colorado River.

Hite (139) **Hite Marina** gets its name from Cass Hite, a former prospector who settled in Ticaboo canyon, and built a town called "Hite City" on the banks of the Colorado River at the mouth of Trachyte Canyon. He and his brothers ran a store and a small post office, and sold provisions and supplies to the many miners who came to Glen Canyon. He irrigated the land around the town and had many fruit trees, grapes, and watermelons. The current-day Hite Marina is two miles downstream from the Dirty Devil drainage.

Dirty Devil River (141) The Dirty Devil River was named by John Wesley Powell's crew on their first journey in 1869. They made camp there at the mouth on July 28, 1869. Powell's crew noticed the small stream was "exceedingly muddy and has an unpleasant odor." William Dunn, when asked by another crewmember if it was a trout stream, answered that it was "a dirty devil." The Dirty Devil heads at Fish Lake, then picks up the Muddy River near Hanksville. It flows toward Lake Powell and joins it at mile 141, just north of Hite Marina.

*   *   *   *   *

As water levels have dropped since 1999, Hite has pretty much become the end of Lake Powell. However, remember that Lake Powell is *186 miles long*, according to most maps and literature, and Hite is at 139. So if you choose to head upstream from Hite, exercise caution. It may not be deep enough for some boats to safely pass through. You certainly can't take a houseboat up there at this time. Make sure you've got a spare propeller or two and the tools to change out your prop, should you decide to venture upriver. You're also not allowed to camp in Cataract Canyon or beyond—those beaches are reserved for river runners.

Narrow Canyon (141-145) This was called Narrow Canyon by John Wesley Powell as the walls closed in very close. When Lake Powell is full, the lake funnels up Narrow Canyon and beyond. This is not a branching canyon, but the very corridor that the Colorado River flows through.

Rock Canyon (143) This is a small canyon off Narrow Canyon, named for obvious features. There is also a "grainery rock" reportedly located at the head of the canyon.

Mille Crag Bend (146-149) This is a large bend in the Colorado River, and was named by John Wesley Powell for the countless number of crags, pinnacles, and interesting rock formations.

Sheep Canyon (148) This canyon was named for the petroglyph of a desert bighorn sheep, which was found in the middle of a cliff in the canyon.

Freddies Cistern (150) This small canyon contained several small waterpockets in the rocks. Just who "Freddie" was remains to be seen. It is possible that Powell's second expedition in 1871 had named it for Frederick Dellenbaugh, a member of that expedition.

Cataract Canyon (156-162) This is a long section of the Colorado River canyon that is narrow and full of drops and rapids. John Wesley Powell named it as such on his first voyage in 1869.

Cove Canyon (151.5) This canyon was first called "Big Cove Canyon" by David D. Rust in 1935. Otis "Dock" Marston noted in 1974 that coves weren't just by the river, but further up the canyon as well.

Dark Canyon (153) This canyon was named by ranchers for being deep and dark near the mouth of the canyon.

Rockfall Canyon (154) This canyon was named for a large rockfall that tumbled down from the rim of the canyon.

Bowdie Canyon (161) It is rumored that this canyon is either named for an outlaw, a cowboy, or a miner named "Bowdie." There is also a Bowdie Point nearby to the north, overlooking the Colorado River corridor.

Clearwater Canyon (162) Powell's second expedition (1871-72) called this canyon "Eden Canyon" as it was such a paradise in the desert.

Ellsworth Kolb of the William R. Chenoweth USGS Expedition of 1921 wanted to call it "Chenoweth Canyon," but Chenoweth himself overruled Kolb and called it "Clearwater Canyon."

Easter Pasture Canyon (163) According to Ned Chaffin, a relative of his by the name of Faun Chaffin first found his way into the canyon on an Easter Sunday, so the name stuck.

Palmer Canyon (165) In the 1940s this canyon was called "John Palmer Canyon" by a team of archaeologists from a museum in Pittsburgh. They were exploring looking for ruins. John David "Johnny" Palmer (1893-1953) was a cowboy who worked for the Scorup/Somerville and TY Cattle companies.

Gypsum Canyon (167) This canyon was named by John Wesley Powell for the "great amounts of gypsum" observed there after a flash flood in 1869.

Calf Canyon (169) This canyon was also called "Waterhole Canyon" on previous maps. It later became known as Calf Canyon since cattlemen would keep the calves in this canyon when they were weaning them.

Imperial Canyon (170) According to John Scorup, this canyon was a "big, lush, majestic valley. Like a king's."

End of Lake Powell (172) Boundary of Glen Canyon National Recreation Area.

*   *   *   *   *

As John Wesley Powell made his historic Colorado River voyages for science from 1869 to 1872, he was able to map a large blank spot that had been unknown to the rest of the nation. Powell had discovered and named the last mountain range to be found in the continental United States, the Henry Mountains. Powell named the five-peak Henry range for his friend and mentor, Joseph Henry. The Henry Mountains officially appeared on maps on May 3, 1872. This small range is situated toward the north end of Lake Powell. It contains five peaks in elevation from 7,930 to 11,522 feet. The five peaks are:

Mt. Holmes	7,930	Named for William Henry Holmes, a geologist
Mt. Ellsworth	8,235	Named for Col. Ephraim Ellsworth (?)
Mt. Hillers	10,723	Named for John K. (Jack) Hillers, a photographer
Mt. Pennell	11,371	Named for Joseph Pennell, an illustrator
Mt. Ellen	11,522	Named for Ellen Powell Thompson, Powell's sister

Powell named each peak for family and friends. However, there is nothing definitive about the naming of Mt. Ellsworth. Grove Karl Gilbert, a scientist on the Powell survey of the Henry Mountains, used the name "Mt. Ellsworth" in 1875. It is surmised that Powell named the mountain for Col. Ephraim Ellsworth, one of the first Union Officers to die in the Civil War.

Grove Karl Gilbert was the first to truly study the Henry Mountains, and was the first to describe them as "laccoliths" in the mid-1870s. Laccoliths are volcanic igneous intrusions through the sandstone of the Colorado Plateau, much like Navajo Mountain, at the south end of Lake Powell.

It is also interesting to note that John Wesley Powell mingled with and respected all Indian tribes he came into contact with during his journeys, learning much from each culture. The Piute Indians referred to Powell as "Ka-Pu-Rats," which meant "he who is missing an arm." This name the Piutes gave to Powell is very similar to another feature in Lake Powell country—the *Kaiparowits* Plateau. Similarities aside, Kaiparowits is a Piute word meaning "big mountain's little brother." On Powell's second Colorado River voyage in 1872, his brother-in-law, Almon Thompson, came along as the chief of the land-based survey. Thompson named the 80-mile long plateau "Kaiparowits" on May 30, 1872, likely in honor of his Major brother-in-law.

Millions of people worldwide have come to know and love Lake Powell over the past five decades, but there are a few for whom Lake Powell has long been a thorn in their side. These are the few who would rather see Lake Powell emptied. They claim that Powell's water could be more efficiently stored downstream in Lake Mead. Don't let this notion fool you. Lake Mead sits at a much lower elevation, has higher temperatures, and has double the evaporation rate of Lake Powell. So it only makes sense that both lakes, Powell and Mead, are equally important to water supplies in the west. Both are needed.

Still, others have thought that Lake Powell should be drained and the water stored *underground* in aquifers. That would certainly solve the evaporation problem, which is normal for any body of water, but when water is underground, it can go anywhere. Who are we to think that we could control water staying put underground? How could we be sure that it doesn't get contaminated underground? There are so many unknowns and variables. Besides, the human race has a very real need for recreation, and millions of people choose to recreate on water—we have that right and we have that freedom. Humans, by nature, are drawn to water. We can't boat underground. We can't fish underground. We can't enjoy water if it's underground.

Drought has tested Lake Powell since 1999, lowering the lake level down to 1/3 capacity. The lowest measurement taken since the lake filled in 1980 was 3555.10 on Friday, April 8th, 2005. However, with dwindling flows and less water coming down the Colorado River in the first two decades of the 2000s, Lake Powell's water level has achieved a new low, ending the Water Year 2021 at 3545.46. With concerns about dropping water levels in many lakes in the western U.S., the states are going to have to work together to come up with solutions to better manage our waterways. A challenge for sure, since pretty much every area of the west is experiencing growth in population.

Each year environmental groups who wish to see the demise of Lake Powell state that Powell is naturally draining away, and the long-term forecast for water will not improve, according to their computer models. However, for the optimists, we see a different picture. Lake Powell was designed to fluctuate with annual water flows. With a few good, wet years, Lake Powell could feasibly fill again to 3700. When the plentiful precipitation returns again, Lake Powell will be ready and willing to contain it.

Lake Powell's entire purpose was for the Upper Basin states to have a storage reservoir so they could meet their yearly downstream water delivery to the Lower Basin states. Period. And the system is working beautifully. In the dry years of the early 2000s, Lake Powell was able to deliver the annual 8.23 million acre-feet downstream, despite the drought. Could you imagine how millions in the west would have fared without Lake Powell?

Because we have the Colorado River system of reservoirs, the west has been able to grow and thrive. So how do we move into the future of water in the west, as the populations steadily grow? Water will always flow down the Colorado; some years will have plentiful water able to meet the downstream delivery, and some years will not. Water managers have surely gotten better at managing the system. Now, more than ever before, the western United States needs to get their priorities in order by cutting back on excessive water usage, since droughts are now commonplace.

* * * * *

Even though the *Wild Red River* of the Colorado has been tamed, Lake Powell can still be a place of extreme danger as she throws her storm-laden tantrums. Most people leave Lake Powell taking wonderful memories with them, of perfect, restful vacations. Some have harrowing stories to tell, and on the extreme end, lives are even lost. What follows is a simple list that all Lake Powell visitors should heed, no matter if you're on a luxury 75-foot houseboat, or a 10-foot aluminum fishing boat. Be prepared, use some common sense, and expect anything. You'll be better equipped to handle any situation and minimize damage or injuries.

- Children 12 and under need to wear life jackets at all times around and on the water. It's the law! Besides, babies and toddlers don't float.

- Dogs must be leashed on docks and at marinas. Clean up and dispose of dog waste properly. Don't leave it on the beaches.

- Apply sunscreen often. Drink plenty of water.

- Wear light colored breathable clothing that will block harmful UV rays.

- Don't walk barefoot on beaches. There may be broken glass in the sand. And by the way, *don't* break bottles or any other glass and leave them on the beaches! A cut foot can quickly ruin a vacation.

- Don't be the person with "ramp rage" before launching your vessel. You're at Lake Powell to relax and enjoy it. Don't embarrass and humiliate yourself. Things can and will go wrong, best to keep a cool head.

- Give a wide berth when passing other vessels—don't "buzz" them just because you have a bigger or more expensive boat. Be a courteous boater. Give at least 100 feet of space as you pass. Think of the large wake your boat might give off, and if it might swamp a smaller boat.

- Fireworks are ILLEGAL. Period. There are very small signs stating so at each marina, but they are there. Leave your explosives at home. Fireworks are also LITTER.

- Graffiti is also ILLEGAL. Don't scratch or carve anything into the sandstone. It desecrates the natural scenery. Penalties for violators include fines of up to $5,000 and/or six months in jail. The phone number to report violators is: 800-582-4351. If you feel you must leave your mark, do it with the clamshells you find on the beach, build a sandcastle, or better yet, spell it out in driftwood or rocks.

- When hiking, don't go in the heat of mid-summer. If you do, don't plan any extensive hikes, unless you can bring a gallon or more of water. Always bring water on hikes. Some of the best months to hike are March, April, and October. Don't hike by yourself, unless you tell others of your destination and expected arrival time.

- Cliff jumping sure is great fun, but it's illegal to jump off anything higher than 15 feet. Only jump into water that you can see there are no sub-surface rocks. Don't be a statistic of drowning victims. NPS does not condone cliff jumping at any level.

- Select a campsite that is off the main channel—you'll want good protection from wind and sudden storms. Never camp in a dry wash that could flood in a storm. Don't park your boat under a storm pour-off where water will cascade from the rim of the canyon.

- If you're in a boat when a windstorm comes on, first get your life jacket on, and then get to a secluded back canyon immediately to ride out the storm. DO NOT try to keep going in the storm. Each year, boats have swamped with water in storms and SUNK. If there is a high-wind forecast for the day you want to be on the water, best not to even go at all.

- Don't camp close to neighboring boats, unless you know them.

- Keep music turned down—it travels and amplifies across the water. Your neighbors probably don't want to hear your music all night long. Be courteous. 10:00pm is quiet hours, so music and generators should power down at that time.

- Don't run your generator *all night long.* If you need air conditioning that badly, why not try sleeping on the top of the houseboat under the stars? It's the best.

- Porta Potties are required, unless you're camping very close to a marina. There are also eight floating restrooms around the lake. If you have a houseboat, USE the bathroom on the houseboat. NEVER leave human waste on the beach. As water levels rise, no one wants to be swimming in human waste.

- Did you know you're only supposed to have a campfire in a fire pan? Yet, campfire rings exist all over the beaches. If you don't have a fire pan, use an existing ring. But DON'T burn cans or bottles in the fire pit. They don't burn! Pack them out with the garbage. Collapse the fire ring when you leave your camp. Cigarette butts are litter too. Pack them out; don't leave them on the beach.

- Secure all garbage, locked away. Ravens will always try to get into the garbage while you're away from your camp or boat. Should you fail to stow the garbage, you'll have a mess to clean when you return.

- Anchor boats properly, either by burying anchors, or using large rocks to tie up to. NEVER stake anything into the sandstone. Stakes left poking out are a danger to people and boats.

- If you have a marine radio, pay attention to channels 1 and 16. Weather forecasts continually broadcast on channel 1, and channel 16 is for hailing.

- Wear polarized sunglasses to help you see what's just below the surface of the water. With continually changing water levels, you'll want to watch for rocks just beneath the surface. Pay attention to buoys that warn of rocks and other underwater strata.

- Pack out what you pack in. This is perhaps the **ONE** golden rule. Leave your beach cleaner than you found it. Take only pictures, leave only footprints. Kill nothing but time.

* * * * *

Below Glen Canyon Dam ~ The Grand Canyon

By Tiffany Mapel

"The song of the river ends not at her banks but in the hearts of those who have loved her."

~ Buffalo Joe

If you're ever in Page, Arizona and you've got a few extra hours, go to the Carl Hayden Visitor Center at the Dam, and sign up for a Glen Canyon Dam tour. It takes about an hour, and it's well worth it. You can call (928) 608- 6072 to book a tour. It costs $5 for adults, 17 and over. Children 7 to 16 are $2.50, and children under 6 are free. Your tour guide will talk you through history as you walk over and through the Dam. It is an impressive piece of engineering, to say the least.

At the end of the tour you can look from the Dam, downstream into Glen Canyon. A world-class trout fishery exists below the Dam, and includes the stretch of the 15 miles to Lees Ferry. European immigrants, bringing their sport fish with them, introduced rainbow and brown trout into the Colorado River, long before any of the dams were put in place. If fishing is your thing, guides are available to take you fishing below the dam in the trophy waters.

You can also book a float trip from the Dam to Lees Ferry. It will take a few hours, and is another worthwhile side trip to do while in Page. There are no rapids between the Dam and Lees Ferry. It's a nice, easy float with a small amount of hiking too. Near the "Horseshoe Bend," a panel of impressive pictographs can be seen, not far from the river.

Lees Ferry is the dividing point between the Upper and Lower Basins of the Colorado River drainage. Under current legislation, the Upper Basin is obligated to release 8.23 million acre feet of water to the Lower Basin each water year, which runs from October 1st to September 30th of each year. Back in 1776, explorers Dominguez and Escalante tried to ford the river at Lees Ferry, but could not get across. They had to head upstream, and eventually crossed at the "Crossing of the Fathers." Later, in 1871 with financing from the Mormon Church, John D. Lee built a ferry at Lees Ferry. Because it was close to the Paria River drainage, it was originally called "Paria Crossing." In the summer of 1872 when John Wesley Powell returned to finish his second journey down the Colorado River, John D. Lee was opening his ferry. The original site of Lees Ferry was actually one-half mile upstream from the current boat launch ramp. On survey maps of 1921, mile zero is fixed at the original ferry site. John D. Lee was executed by firing squad in 1877 for his role in the Mountain Meadows Massacre back in 1857. His wife, Emma Lee, continued to run the ferry service. In 1879 she sold the ferry back to the Mormon Church for 100 milk cows. The Church continued to operate the Ferry until 1910. The Ferry was ultimately closed in 1929 when the Navajo Bridge was completed over Marble Canyon six miles downstream.

Commercial and private raft trips through the Grand Canyon put in at Lees Ferry. You have the option of either motorized or float trips. Motorized trips will take from 3 to 5 days, and float trips can run from 12 to 18 days, or more. While any time spent in the Grand Canyon is worth it, I highly recommend taking the float trip. Slow down to the speed of the water, and observe your surroundings. Take your time to *see.*

Back in 2005, a group of 20 friends and family from Durango, Colorado got the opportunity of a lifetime: a 12-day float trip down the Grand Canyon. We booked our Grand Canyon trip about 8 months in advance with a commercial outfitter based in Flagstaff, Arizona. (I've heard that private trips have to wait at least 10 years before their turn comes up. Now they're on a lottery-system, and I'm not sure how long the wait is for a private trip). What follows is a report of the journal I kept during our trip, July 12-24, 2005.

Day 1, July 12th, Tuesday
We were all excited on the bus from Flagstaff, anticipating our big GRAND trip. We were finally going to see the Canyon from the bottom up, instead of looking down from the rim. It was going to be a whole new perspective. The bus stopped in Cameron, Arizona for a rest stop at one of the largest trading posts on the reservation, but I was eager to get going. Later, as we approached the Canyon, the bus driver let us out to walk over Navajo Bridge, looking down on the Colorado River. We also passed by many Native American artisans, who were selling their jewelry and wares near the bridge. When we got to Lees Ferry, our guides were busy rigging our boats: five 18-foot inflatable oar boats, and one 18-foot inflatable paddle-boat. The guides are experts at loading everything: food, dry bags, gear, and "groovers"—the portable toilets. Everything is strapped down securely. After a brief orientation from our guides, they passed out life jackets, which we were all responsible for during our trip, and we launched from Lees Ferry on a 48-degree Colorado River in the summer sun. This is the beginning, mile 0, and the start of Marble Canyon. We had nice smooth water, and it was clear blue-green. We had lunch at a small sandy beach under the Navajo Bridge, and watched the condors in the girders of the Bridge high above. The great, endangered birds have been reintroduced in the area, and are making quite a comeback. When beaching anywhere in the Canyon, you cannot leave any trace; all scraps of food are picked up, and everything is packed with you. Rapids that day were Badger Creek, Soap Creek, and House Rock. Big waves, and we all got a

good drenching. First camp was at mile 20. While a few opt to use a tent, most of us sleep right on the beach—lay down a tarp, a "paco pad," sheets and a pillow, and you're good to go. Just don't mind all the critters that might crawl over you—toads, lizards, velvet ants, scorpions... They won't bother you, as long as you don't bother them.

Day 2, July 13th, Wednesday
After a tasty breakfast, (the guides do all the cooking for their trips—how sweet is that?) we went through North Canyon Rapid, and then hiked up North Canyon. There was a small pool at the end with amazing reflections. No one disturbed the water, as we were taking turns getting the perfect reflection picture with still water. We saw plenty of frogs, toads, and tadpoles in the water. That day we hit the "Roaring 20s" rapids: 21, 23, 23 ½, 24, 24 ½, 25, Cave Springs, 27 (Tiger Wash), and 29. Rolling waves, and we all felt more confident in the rapids. We saw what was left of an old river runner's boat, which was chained to the shore a mile or so after 24 ½ rapid. Bert Loper, the "Old Man of the Colorado," reportedly had a heart attack and died on July 8, 1949 as he went through that rapid, and his body was never found. His boat was eventually found 15 miles downstream. Bert was one of the Colorado River's pioneers, as far as running rapids goes. We camped that evening on an expansive beach just past South Canyon. We could look downstream at Stanton's Cave and Vasey's Paradise. My husband, Frank, went fly-fishing and caught a few Rainbow Trout. A lone bighorn sheep browsed the ledges above our camp, unfazed by us. Bighorn sheep are all over the Grand Canyon. You will see them frequently. Just after sunset, a hot wind swept down the canyon.

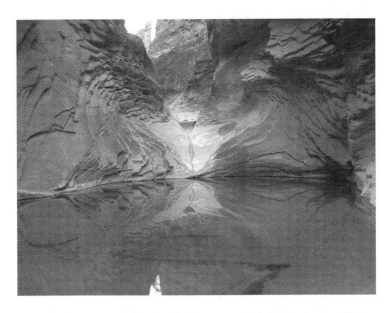

North Canyon pool, Marble Canyon. T. Mapel photo, 2005.

Day 3, July 14th, Thursday

That morning, three small scorpions were found in a life jacket. We made sure to shake everything out before we packed our dry bags. We left camp, and went one mile down to Redwall Cavern. Just before the Cavern, Vasey's Paradise greeted us on the right wall. Water bursts out of the Redwall Limestone in three or four places, and cascades on down to the river. It is lush with greenery and columbines and monkey flowers. There is also a population of endangered Kanab Amber Snails living there, so we were not permitted to land at Vasey's Paradise. Instead, our guides slowed the boats as we all took pictures and admired the green paradise within the rocky canyon. When we got to Redwall Cavern, we pulled the boats onto the sand, and explored the huge undercut in the Redwall Limestone. One of our guides showed us how to "walk on the moon"—leaning backward, looking up at the ceiling, and running toward the back of the cavern. We found a nest of baby birds in the back. Another guide pointed out a crinoid fossil in a split of some fallen rock. Later, we boated down to 34 ½, "Nautaloid Canyon." Our guide poured water on the rocks so we could see the many Nautaloid fossils. With millions of years of history, the Grand Canyon contains many layers of fossils.

Downstream we hit 36 mile rapid, and saw the old Marble Canyon Dam sites around mile 40. They had drilled into the walls at various places, and some marks were painted on the walls. Then we went through President Harding Rapid at 43 ½. We camped that evening at mile 47—Saddle Canyon. We hiked up through the canyon, which had a nice trail through redbud and fragrant willows, and saw a waterfall, pool, tadpoles, and frogs. It was so peaceful and serene. I could have spent the entire summer in that spot. We saw a very interesting geologic formation high upon a wall—the "Devonian River Channels." There were three of them, and you could clearly see where the old river channels were during the Devonian Period, before the next layer filled them in. Such fascinating geologic history we encounter with each canyon we explore.

Nice beach upstream from Vasey's Paradise, Marble Canyon.
T. Mapel photo, 2005.

Day 4, July 15th, Friday

Today was a pleasant float with many fun riffles. Not quite rapids, but exciting water nonetheless. We went through Nankoweap Rapid. We saw the Indian granaries from the river, but did not hike up to them. (Would have been a hot one!) This is one of the most scenic of overlooks on the Colorado River. You see this view looking downstream from the granaries on Grand Canyon pamphlets frequently. Then we hit Kwagunt Rapid, which was one of my favorites. It had big waves and nice rollers over a fairly large hole. We had lunch on a cool Tapeats shelf in the shade, and then went down to the Little Colorado River tributary. Another trip was there ahead of us. What we saw when we pulled up the tributary a short distance was amazingly clear Caribbean-blue water. The water in the Little Colorado bubbles out of Blue Spring, 13 miles up from the confluence. It is colored by the Calcium Carbonate it contains. It was the most beautiful water I had ever seen. And the water was the perfect temperature—like a giant swimming pool! We hiked up a bit, and immediately hit the current of small rapids. Wearing our life jackets on our butts, we bumped our way down the travertine "rapids." The guides snorkeled around looking for treasures, while we made trains floating the rapid, and enjoyed the afternoon in the water. We did many laps, and I could have stayed there all day. We made camp that evening around mile 64. We are now officially in Grand Canyon. Camp that evening was pretty exciting. Frank and I explored up a small wash behind our camp. We weren't very far up when we heard what we thought was a rockslide coming down. Frank stopped me, and we listened to see where it was coming from. Suddenly, a herd of stampeding bighorn sheep rounded the corner and looked at us. They paused, and then quickly climbed the walls out of the canyon above us. Very exciting! We wondered what was chasing them? We didn't stick around to find out. Back at camp, as twilight fell upon the Canyon, a large school of Humpback Chubs played near the shore. We checked out their strange shapes and marveled at the endangered native fish that circled like sharks. At dark, a motorboat pulled up with two guys from Arizona Game & Fish. They were doing scientific experiments, shocking fish, (trout) and checking on the Chub populations. We watched them shock fish for a bit before we all retired to our sleeping bags. A great day on the river!

Day 5, July 16th, Saturday
Today was a huge day of rapids! The scenery changed with the variety of rock layers, as we all got a geology lesson. We hit Chuar

Rapid first, then Tanner. We stopped above Unkar Rapid at mile 72 to hike around what the guides called "Furnace Flats" to see some ruins and potsherds. Fascinating history in a beautiful area. It was a hot day, but the cold spray from the river felt great. Finally, we run Unkar Rapid, then Nevills, Hance, Sockdolager, Grapevine, and 83 mile. We pulled the boats in to hike up Clear Creek, and this is the place with the blistering hot Schist we had to climb to get above to Clear Creek. The rock was intensely hot, and you could see the heat waves rising from it. I really wished I had a pair of thick, leather gloves. It was a challenging hike over the hot, jagged rock, but Clear Creek was worth it. The water in the creek felt refreshing. At the top, we see the "Horizontal Waterfall"—where the water hits a pocket in the rock, and shoots out sideways. We spent some time there, and then headed back to the boats. We concluded the day with a run through Zoroaster Rapid and camped at Cremation Creek near mile 86.

"Horizontal Waterfall" in Clear Creek, Grand Canyon.
T. Mapel photo, 2005.

Day 6, July 17th, Sunday

We floated the two miles down to Phantom Ranch. Some of us hiked up to mail postcards and purchase t-shirts and lemonade. Bright Angel Creek runs along the trail, and it was beautiful up there. Phantom Ranch looks like a great place for tired hikers to spend the day relaxing. A mule train went by, probably to go pick up tourists for a ride in the canyon. Back at the boats, it was another exciting day of rapids. We hit Pipe Springs, Horn Creek, Salt Creek, Granite, Hermit (got doused!), Boucher, Crystal (scouted first, then never even got wet), Tuna Creek, Agate, Sapphire, Turquoise, 104 (Emerald), Ruby, Serpentine, and Bass. We pulled in soaking wet to hike Shinumo Creek for another waterfall and a swim. Stayed there a while, enjoying the afternoon. Most of the side canyons that contain flowing creeks have much warmer water than the Colorado River. Native fish called "Speckled Dace" abound in the side creeks. They are small—about five inches, and they will come up to you if you sit still in the water. After our Shinumo visit we hit two more rapids--Shinumo, and 110 mile, and we make camp at 110.

Day 7, July 18th, Monday

A few fun riffles and rapids today, like Hakatai and Waltenberg. We hiked up to Elves Chasm—another gorgeous waterfall—quite possibly the most picturesque place in all of Grand Canyon. A few brave souls jump from the top into the cooler water. Downstream, we hit more rapids: Blacktail, Forster, Fossil, 128, Specter, Bedrock, and Dubendorff. We pull in to hike Stone Creek. Yet another beautiful waterfall to stand in, and small pools to lounge in. The Grand Canyon is full of waterfalls! Camped that evening above Tapeats Creek, near 133 1/2. Big hike tomorrow up to Thunder River.

Elves Chasm, Grand Canyon. T. Mapel photo, 2005.

Approaching Bedrock Rapid, Grand Canyon. T. Mapel photo, 2005.

Day 8, July 19th, Tuesday

We get going early after making lunches for the day. Eleven of us are hiking to Thunder River, a 3 1/2 mile hike up, and the rest are going to Deer Creek and the "Patio." The hike up takes two hours, and we go along Tapeats Creek for much of it. We jump in the cooler water, and ride a small rapid. Parts of the Thunder River hike are steep, so we take our time. Most of our hike up is in the shade, so that helped. One of our guides pointed out some Purple Sage, which had the most amazing, alluring scent of anything in the canyon. Finally, we can see where Thunder River bursts out of a few holes in the Muav layer, just under the Redwall Limestone. Thunder River is aptly named. It roars and cascades down a mossy incline, creating a cool misty wind. We stay for two hours resting by the cool water, the thunderous sound, and we even drink the cold, pure water. Very refreshing! We fill all our bottles and Camelbacks for the hike down. The hike back is hotter, so we jump in Tapeats Creek again. We get wet at every chance we see. Back at the boats, we head downriver to Deer Creek Falls, a 100-foot waterfall plunging down and visible from the river. Before we get there, we see something white on the water. Thinking it was debris, it turns out to be a white Pelican! He must have wandered up from Mexico. Finally we see Deer Creek Falls. We hike up to see it, and find the rest of our group there. The force of a 100-foot waterfall creates a rush of wind so strong that we can't actually stand beneath the waterfall. For fear of missing anything else, we then hike up to the "Patio," a neat slot canyon in the (Tapeats? Muav?) where Deer Creek runs through. We see a few chuckwalla lizards here. Lizards of all kinds are all over the Grand Canyon. We spend some time at the Patio, and then we all go back to the boats. We camp at mile 137 1/2 on a great beach (all the beaches have been great!), and we notice that the river water is getting warmer. Ahhhh....

Day 9, July 20, Wednesday
We left camp and faced Doris Rapid. She drenched us. Then onto Fishtail, and Kanab Creek Rapids. We stop in Olo Canyon to explore, and also to take a nice mid-morning nap. A small waterfall plunges down onto rock rubble. One guide said it used to be a nice 15-foot deep pool. Must have filled in after a flash flood. Some of the group took a mud bath and washed off in the waterfall. Then it was on to Matkatamiba Canyon for more R and R. There was a neat slot canyon that we all had to climb up to reach another "patio." The guides assisted us, as we had to shimmy up the wall in places. At the top, the stream trickled through various pools, and we spent a few hours there napping and enjoying the sounds of the canyon. It was so silent and still, save for the sweet trickling water sound. The air was considerably cooler than the main canyon. This place was definitely nature's meditative spa! Back at the river, we run Matkatamiba, Upset, and Sinyala Rapids. Very fun! It seems the rapids get bigger the further down river you go. We camp at 155 1/2, and have hot wind, rain, lightning, and thunder in the evening. Not one of us takes shelter. The rain feels too good.

Enjoying Matkatamiba Canyon in Grand Canyon. T. Mapel photo, 2005.

Day 10, July 21, Thursday

Went down to Havasu Creek today. Got an early start, and hiked up. Great weather, and hiking in the shade. What a gorgeous canyon, and inviting warm water too. More Calcium Carbonate in this water, like the Little Colorado. The Havasupai Indians live at the head of Havasu Creek at Supai, about 17 miles away. The hike up to the large pool was about 3 miles. If someone didn't want to go that far, they could stop off anywhere at their own personal pool. A few did so, but I was in the crowd who wanted to see it all, so up I went. Not a bad hike, and we were rewarded after three miles with a large clear pool, and small waterfall, "Beaver Falls." If we would have gone further, we would have reached Mooney Falls, and then Havasu Falls, but we didn't have that much time. Our guides snorkeled around looking for treasures again, while some of us jumped off high and low rocks. The guides called the waterfall "The Tumbler," and it was so entertaining to play in. You jump into the seam where the falls hit the water, curl up into a ball, and the water tumbles you all around and spits you out downstream. Very fun! We ate lunch on the ledges above the pool, and stayed for a few hours before hiking back down the canyon. It was hotter on the way back, so of course, we had to jump in every large pool we saw. We got back to the mouth of Havasu Creek, and saw the black stormy skies northeast of us. Our guides wanted to get going, to avoid being caught in any possible flash flood. With everyone back on the boats, we got safely along downriver, hitting Havasu, 164, and Fern Glen Rapids. A few fun riffles too. We're all really tired tonight, and we're all in bed at dark.

Day 11, July 22, Friday
Ah, a lazy float today with many water fights. The river water is much warmer, and very refreshing to jump into. We get down to Lava Falls to scout it before we make our run. It is HUGE. Thunder River has nothing on this one. We decide to run right, but the right run looks big. The guide on the boat I am in instructs us to hunker down when she says "*Big hit!*" and to hit the "*High Side*" if the boat needs it. We go one boat at a time, and our lead guide films from a rock on the right. Frank sustains a black eye and a lost sunglass lens in a huge wave. Everyone stays in the boats, and we cheer our success. Then my boat goes. Our guide screams, "Big hit!" and I duck in the front of the boat. A big wave washes over us, and fills the front of the boat. We seem to be floating in it, as the boat slowly bails. With the boat full of water, we slowed down considerably. We hit some big rolling waves, and Lava makes sure we're all wet. What a fun rapid! We pull into an eddy to watch the final boat's run. It was certainly a very exciting, nail-biting moment, but the boat comes through and everyone has stayed in the boat. We pull in for lunch on some Tapeats ledges just downstream from Lava. We celebrate with some cold river-temperature beers and a hearty lunch. Then we all take a quick nap after all that adrenaline earlier. I fell completely asleep on the rocky ledge near the river, and when I awoke looking at clouds in the sky, I was briefly lost as to where I was. It was an amazing feeling. What a great place to be. More lazy floating after Lava, and I get to row a few miles on some flat water, and then down Whitmore Rapid. We make camp at 190, and the hot wind hits. Then the rain, lightning, and thunder. We are all piled in the kitchen area,

trying to get snacks and dinner going in the rain. Once again, the rain feels great. The storm passes, and all is peaceful.

Day 12, July 23rd, Saturday

Another lazy river day, drifting through the most scenic place on the planet. One of our guides played her violin, adding a soundtrack that fit perfectly with our day. We had some fun rapids today--205, 209, and 217. I think these numbered rapids need to get names—they're more memorable with names. We swam Three Springs Rapid at 215 1/2, since it was safe. We jumped off a rock from about 12 feet up with our life jackets on, and floated the rapid. The water felt great, and I didn't want to get out. Camped at 220.

Day 13, July 24th, Sunday

Our last day. This morning, the river was running a rich chocolaty brown. I wonder which drainage upstream had flash flooded earlier? We were really lucky to have blue-green water for almost the entire trip. Another leisurely float the last five miles down to Diamond Creek. We stopped and tied up in a rocky eddy to waste time, so we didn't get there too early. We tried to convince our guides to just bypass Diamond Creek and go all the way to Lake Mead. None of us wanted to leave. Later and reluctantly, we reached the Diamond Creek take-out, and started to de-rig and deflate the boats. The sky was cloudy and the air was cool, remnants of Hurricane Emily, we found out. So in case of a flash flood, we had to get away from the river and up to a higher spot to have lunch. We ate the last of our lunch supply, and we were all sad our river journey had to end. We just wanted to stay on the river and keep going. The bus ride up Diamond Creek (which was flowing) was exciting. We got stuck in sand, and had to be pulled out by the boat truck. On the road to Seligman, AZ (which was celebrating Seligman Days) we napped and prepared for the onslaught of song that evening at dinner. It's very different being on a bus going 55 mph, when we've been going about three to four miles per hour for the past 12 days. The bus seemed really fast and reckless to me, and I was resistant to rejoin civilization. Back in Flagstaff, we cleaned up and packed our bags. We all went out for dinner, where our guides planned to join us. It was a jovial dinner, complete with songs and awards. What an amazing trip through the Grand Canyon, and I can't wait to do it all again.

*   *   *   *   *

If you're considering booking a Grand Canyon trip with a commercial outfitter, you won't be disappointed. They are all expert river guides, and know the Canyon's history. The guides also know each and every rapid, and the best and safest routes through them, at any water level. It was nice to be in the Canyon with people who knew what they were doing, as we did witness some private trips that didn't fare as well. The Grand Canyon is no place for rookies.

When you do book a trip, your guide company will prepare you well in advance. Everything you bring will have to fit into a fairly small dry bag. If you go during the summer months, not a lot of clothing is needed. However, for the spring and fall trips, you'll likely be wearing a wetsuit or drysuit at all times.

When I go on a Grand Canyon trip again, there are three things I will bring that I wish I knew about in 2005: a water-proof camera, so I can get the drenching shots through the rapids, leather gloves, so I can climb the blistering hot schist without burning my hands, and a snorkel and mask, so I can search for "treasures" and observe fish in the clear waters of the Little Colorado and Havasu Creek.

Due to fluctuations in releases from Glen Canyon Dam, the water through Grand Canyon is like a "tidal" system—it rises and falls. The further you get downstream from the Dam, you quickly lose sense of what the water's doing, whether it's rising or falling. The guides have to know this, in order to tie the boats up to shore. You want to be mindful tying up as the water's rising, as you have to pull the boats well up onto the shore, so they'll be floating where they need to be by morning.

On my trip in 2005, the river flow was around 13,000 to 15,000cfs. On the Canyon walls, you could see evidence of a water line of a flood stage from the past—from flows of 100,000cfs or more. How fortunate we are to have the Grand Canyon, and also Lake Powell—two very different and beautiful desert water habitats. I love them both.

Some opponents of Glen Canyon Dam paint a picture of a dying Grand Canyon, and disappearing beaches—erosion is harming the beaches. One could also argue that *erosion* is why we have the Grand

Canyon in the first place. Opponents also claim the Dam destroyed the Grand Canyon. I wouldn't say that's an accurate assessment— *altered* from its original state, yes, but certainly not destroyed. When I went through in 2005, I witnessed an ecologically healthy, vibrant Canyon. The plants and animals in the Canyon have adapted, and the whole place seemed in harmony to me. The beaches were also plentiful, enormous, and beautifully kept. We never had to camp on rocks for lack of a good beach. It appeared that everyone was doing his or her part to "pack out what you pack in." I was very impressed. I'm very glad the Marble Canyon Dam and the Bridge Canyon Dam were never put in the Grand Canyon—the river journey is a special one. If you've never seen the Grand Canyon from the river, I highly recommend the trip. If you do one trip in your lifetime, this should be the one. Go see for yourself what an amazing place it is. It is a true wonder of the world.

*   *   *   *   *

Afterword

We truly hope you've enjoyed this book of Colorado River history, Lake Powell, and the Grand Canyon. These are some of the finest places on the planet, and it is our hope that the public will continue to enjoy these special places for generations to come. With enjoyment of these lands and waterways comes responsibility. Please always do your part to pack out what you pack in, and leave your area cleaner than you found it.

For more information on preserving and protecting Lake Powell, please visit the website of the Friends of Lake Powell: www.lakepowell.org

For NPS information on Lake Powell, please visit: www.nps.gov/glca

For Lake Powell fishing and general information, please visit: www.wayneswords.com

For information on the Glen Canyon Conservancy, please visit: www.canyonconservancy.org.

For information on Lake Powell's concessionaires, please visit: www.lakepowell.com and www.antelopepointlakepowell.com

For information on Lake Powell's current and historic water levels, please visit: http://lakepowell.water-data.com

*   *   *   *   *

Maps

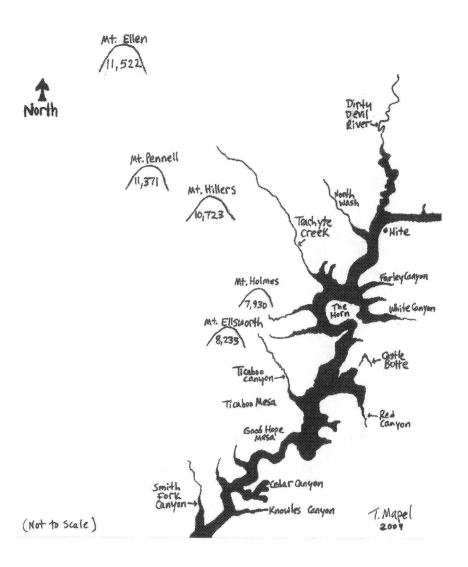

The Henry Mountain Range

Mt. Ellen
11,522

↑
North

Mt. Pennell
11,371

Mt. Hillers
10,723

Dirty Devil River

North Wash

Tachyte Creek

•Hite

Mt. Holmes
7,930

Farley Canyon

White Canyon

The Horn

Mt. Ellsworth
8,239

Castle Butte

Ticaboo Canyon →

Ticaboo Mesa

Red Canyon

Good Hope Mesa

Cedar Canyon

Smith Fork Canyon →

Knowles Canyon

T. Mapel
2009

(Not to Scale)

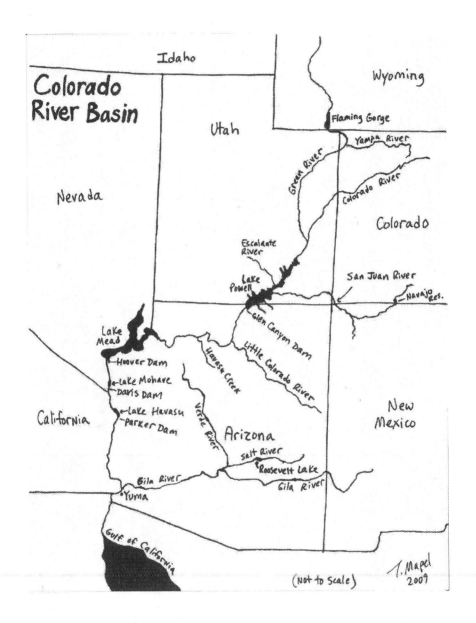

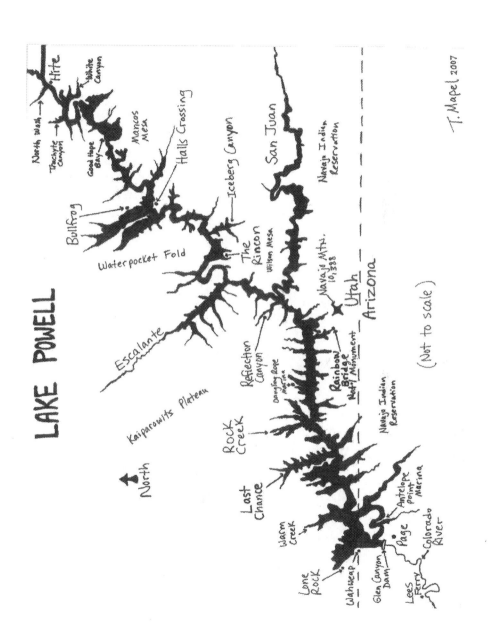

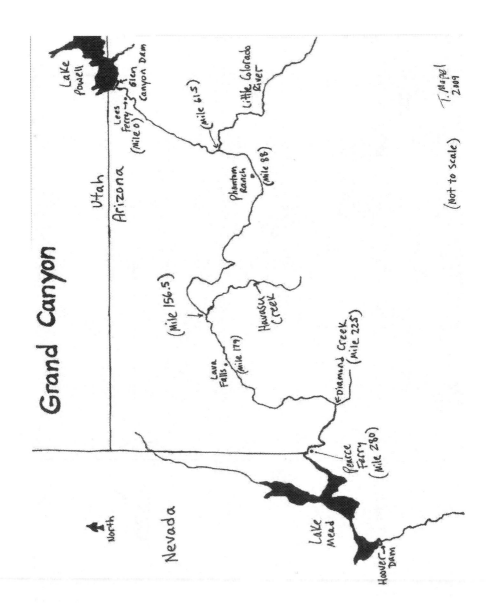

Grand Canyon

North

Nevada

Lake Powell

Utah
Arizona

Lees Ferry (Mile 0)
Glen Canyon Dam

(Mile 61.5)

Little Colorado River

Phantom Ranch (Mile 88)

(Mile 156.5)

Havasu Creek

Lava Falls (Mile 179)

Diamond Creek (Mile 225)

Pearce Ferry (Mile 280)

Lake Mead

Hoover Dam

(Not to Scale)

T. Mapel 2.09

Bibliography

<u>Books</u>

Allen, Steve. <u>Utah's Canyon Country Place Names</u>. Volumes 1 and 2. Durango, CO: Canyon Country Press, 2012.

Belknap, Buzz and Loie Belknap Evans. <u>Grand Canyon River Guide.</u> Evergreen, CO: Westwater Books, 2005.

Crampton, Gregory C. <u>Ghosts of Glen Canyon</u>. Salt Lake City, UT: Tower Productions, 1986.

Crosby, Alexander L. <u>The Colorado Mover of Mountains</u>. Champaign, Il: The Garrard Press, 1961.

Dellenbaugh, Frederick S. <u>A Canyon Voyage.</u> New York, NY: G. P. Putnam's Sons – The Knickerbocker Press, 1908.

Dowler, Warren Leroy and Louise Bishop Dowler. <u>Dowlers Lake Powell Boating Guide</u>. Sierra Madre, California: Dowlers, 1976.

Gaskill, David and Gudy Gaskill, <u>Peaceful Canyon Golden River</u>. Golden, CO: Colorado Mountain Club Press, 2002.

Jones, Stan. <u>Ramblings by Boat and Boot in Lake Powell Country</u>. Page, AZ: Sun Country Publications, 1998.

Kelsey, Michael R. <u>Boater's Guide to Lake Powell</u>. 5th ed. Provo, UT: Kelsey Publishing, 2008.

McCourt, Tom. <u>King of the Colorado The Story of Cass Hite</u>. Price, UT: Southpaw Publications, 2012.

McCourt, Tom. <u>White Canyon</u>. Price, UT: Southpaw Publications, 2003.

Nichols, Tad. <u>Glen Canyon Images of a Lost World</u>. Santa Fe, NM: Museum of New Mexico Press, 1999.

Powell, John Wesley. <u>The Exploration of the Colorado River and its Canyons</u>. New York: Penguin Books, 2003.

Stegner, Wallace. <u>Beyond the Hundredth Meridian</u>. New York: Penguin Books, 1992.

Van Cott, John W. <u>Utah Place Names</u>. Salt Lake City: University of Utah Press, 1990.

Wagoner, Jay. <u>Arizona's Heritage</u>. Salt Lake City: Peregrine Smith Inc., 1978.

Webb, Roy, ed. <u>High, Wide, and Handsome The River Journals of Norman D. Nevills</u>. Logan, UT: Utah State University Press, 2005.

Magazines

Roberts, David. "Finding Everett Ruess." <u>National Geographic Adventure</u>. Apr. 2009: 74-81+. Print.

Maps

<u>Glen Canyon National Recreation Area, Utah-Arizona</u>. Denver, CO: U.S. Geological Survey, 1969.

Jones, Stan, <u>Map of Lake Powell Country</u>, Page, AZ: Sun Country Publications, 2006.

Websites

Bureau of Reclamation,
        http://www.usbr.gov

Coachella Valley Historical Society,
        http://coachellavalleymuseum.org

"Collections & Exhibits." GCC,
https://www.canyonconservancy.org/collections. Accessed 31 Oct. 2021.

Lake Powell water level database
http://lakepowell.water-data.com

McPherson, Robert S.
http://www.media.utah.edu/UHE/s/SANJUANRIVER.html

United States Geological Survey,
http://usgs.gov/125/articles/powell.html

Places Visited

Arizona Historical Society, (http://www.arizonahistoricalsociety.org)
1300 N. College Ave.
Tempe, AZ 85281

John Wesley Powell Museum, (http://www.powellmuseum.org)
#6 N. Lake Powell Blvd.
Page, AZ 86040

Salt River Project History Museum
1521 N. Project Drive
Tempe, AZ 85281-1206

Sharlot Hall Museum, (http://sharlot.org)
415 West Gurley St.
Prescott, AZ 86301

Tucson Library, (http://www.library.pima.gov)
101 N. Stone Ave.
Tucson, AZ 85701

* * * * *

And special thanks to Page, Arizona residents, Paul Ostapuk, for historical information; Wayne Gustaveson, Lake Powell's Fisheries Biologist; and to Steve Ward, for his knowledge, passion, and love for Lake Powell.